TEEN TO TEEN:
Plain Talk From Teens About Sex, Self-Esteem and Everything in Between

Melanie A. Gold, D.O., F.A.A.P., F.A.C.O.P.
Associate Professor of Pediatrics
Department of Pediatrics
Division of Adolescent Medicine
University of Pittsburgh School of Medicine

Mara Horwitz
University of Pennsylvania, 2007

Ashley Greene
Schenley High School, 2005

Abe Taleb
Schenley High School, 2005

Robert A. Hatcher, M.D., M.P.H
Professor of Gynecology and Obstetrics
Emory University School of Medicine

Edited by Rita L. Labbett, B.A.

Illustrations by Raymond Steffins

Additional Photography credits: Rita L. Labbett, B.A.

The Opinions offered in **Teen to Teen** are solely those of the authors.

HOW TO ORDER

Bridging the Gap Communications, Inc.
120 Peachtree Circle NE
Carriage House
Atlanta, GA 30309

Call: 404-875-5001
Fax: 404-875-5030

Order online:
www.ManagingContraception.com

Persona Grata... Thanks!

Vital to the creation of this book have been the following contributors:

Sharon M. Schnare, C.R.N.P.
Rita L. Labbett, B.A.
Karen Derzic, B.A.
Kym A. Smith, B.S., C.C.R.C.
Kristin Delisi, C.R.N.P.
Alexandra Sasha Carey, M.D.
Jacqueline M. Simpronio, B.S.
Jonathan H. Weinberg, M.S.
Aimee J. Hong, B.A.
Patrick W. Blake, B.A.
Teresa Angiolieri, B.S.
Anya V. Sheftel, B.A.
Peggy Gordon, M.P.H.
Kim Davis
Erika Pluhar, PhD

Your help and support have been much appreciated!

TEEN TO TEEN

GETTING HONEST WITH THE YOUNG

We do our worst at sexual misinformation with adolescents. This is when our children are most impressionable on the subject and most hormonally compelled. And what do we tell them? We tell them that there is something wrong with being too interested in sex. We tell them that, above all, they must not engage in any sexual activity until they are older and wise, - like us. For good measure we tell them that if they do engage in sexual activity now, it will ruin them for life.

Thus we manage to turn their natural sexual interest into unwarranted sexual confusion.

Dr. Kennedy Shultz
Minister

Gold

Horwitz

Greene

Taleb

Hatcher

Preface I

Teenagers are extremely curious individuals; we love to ask questions and learn new things. Throughout our adolescent lives we encounter changes that define our characters, values, and goals. During this time, we face many obstacles that may make it difficult to maintain the values and goals we set for ourselves. Some of these obstacles could be drugs, alcohol, school, peers, or sex. In our search to understand these issues, we seek guidance and direction from many different people: coaches, parents, friends, mentors, teachers, and family. Learning how to communicate is the first step in seeking direction from others.

However, the people we turn to for guidance cannot always answer all of our questions; they may not give us accurate answers to our questions. We often feel more comfortable turning to our friends for help, but they are usually just as confused as we are. Without helpful and accurate answers to our questions, we might make unhealthy choices when difficult situations arise. Understanding what to do in these situations can help us better prepare, and therefore become more responsible and healthier individuals.

Teen to Teen is in part a book about relationships, self-respect and sex and how to prevent pregnancy and sexually transmitted diseases in the new millennium. **Quest for Excellence** was written in the early 1990's by a collection of high school and college students who thought it might answer some basic questions that teenagers ask about sex, sexual etiquette, drugs, alcohol, choosing contraceptive methods, and basic questions about growing up. In this new book adapted from **Quest for Excellence**, we have added sections about how to take a step by step approach to success in achieving your goals and how to better cope with stress. We have also updated the health information in the book. We hope that this book helps you learn more about yourself and the world around you, so that you can make the best choices possible for you.

Ashley Greene
Schenley High School, 2005

Abe Taleb
Schenley High School, 2005

Pittsburgh, PA, November 2004

Preface II

My high school experience was not so long ago – and as I look back on those years, I remember all sorts of questions that I asked: How will I have the time and energy to manage all of my classes and activities? What do I want to do after high school? Who are my closest friends? Can I handle a serious relationship right now? What exactly does puberty mean for me, now that the changes are happening in my own body? Who can I trust and ask for help with these concerns??

These are questions that I'm sure a lot of teenagers ask in high school...but they don't stop at graduation! As a college student, I still have many of the same goals, concerns, and questions that I had in high school. Since then, some of these issues have become even more important to me, such as: time management and stress control (balancing classes, activities, friends, and my personal needs), independence and loneliness (being away from home), relationships and reproductive choices (understanding the benefits and risks of sexual activity, and developing serious relationships with other people), and life planning (what kind of education, career, family, and lifestyle I want to have in the future).

Teen to Teen was created because it is often difficult to find reliable and trustworthy answers to these complicated questions. While this book cannot possibly answer all of the questions we have, it can teach us good ways to search for answers – using our natural curiosity, healthy communication, education and information, and guidance from close friends, mentors, and family. I hope that you will find this book useful, both as a source of information as well as a guide on your search for further understanding.

As long as you keep asking questions, you will continue your quest for knowledge, information, responsibility, happiness, and *excellence*. Keep asking, keep reading, and keep questing!

Mara Horwitz
Frick HS '03
University of Pennsylvania '07

Philadelphia, PA, November, 2004

TABLE OF CONTENTS

Part One:

Moving Through Adolescence Into Adulthood

MILESTONES TO MATURITY

The first version of this book was called "Quest for Excellence." What does it mean to be on a "Quest for Excellence?" In general, being on a quest for excellence means striving to do the best you can do in all aspects of your life. Although you will undoubtedly be considering this question throughout your lifetime, your teenage years can be the most exciting and challenging part of your search. Creating your own identity and experiencing your independence is part of your Quest for Excellence. Several thoughtful people have developed four main challenges to become a successful adult. A good way to begin the "Quest for Excellence" is to look at your own life and how you are going to meet these challenges. These might be considered "Milestones to Maturity."

1. Figure out what you want to do when you grow up.
During adolescence, you may begin to think about taking care of yourself rather than having someone else look after you. This gradual change brings you freedom as you make your own decisions about how you want to live; but this change in responsibility can also produce anxiety. However, it is important to make this transition. It will be easier for you to become an independent adult when you are independent of your parents.

Some young adults have an idea of the career they are interested in by the time they finish high school and others might not know exactly what they want to do yet. You may decide that you need more education or experience to figure it out. Education can be a helpful tool for making career choices. As long as you keep an open mind, you are bound to find a career that is right for you, interests you, and will enable you to earn the money you need to be an independent adult.

2. What's right? What's wrong?
Early in life you may be exposed to different value systems from your family, place of worship (church, synagogue, mosque, or other), community, and friends. It is normal, at a young age, to accept some of these values without asking if they are right for you – for example, children often have the same religious and

political beliefs as their parents.   Later, however, you may begin to question these "adopted" value systems and develop your own. Conflict is okay; it shows that you are thinking for yourself, and producing thoughts different from those you learned in childhood. This process of questioning and developing values is an important milestone to maturity and wisdom; it shows that you are thinking and prioritizing as an individual. Because you learn your personal rights and wrongs through experience, value systems are constantly changing during a lifetime.

3. Learn who you are and how to love yourself.
Part of growing up is learning to appreciate yourself just as you are. How are you special and unique? What are you good at? What makes you happy? Are you a good soccer player, dancer, computer whiz, or clarinet player? Do you have a good sense of humor, or do you enjoy other people? How you feel about the qualities that make up your personality influences your identity.

Everyone also develops a gender identity – how a person views him or herself as male or female. Becoming comfortable with your gender may require striking a balance between what society expects of you as a man or woman, and what you expect and want for yourself. Achieving a gender identity is a key part of appreciating yourself the way you are.

You also have a sexual identity, which develops as you discover the people and things that you find sexually and physically attractive. This may change and develop over time, and many people experiment with different sexual identities in a lifetime.

4. Learn to see your parents as people, not just as parents.
You probably grew up believing that your parents were perfect, and then realized later on that they were not. Finding this out can be very difficult, but realizing that your parents are not perfect allows you to view them as real people. And once you can see your parents as people, you can also see them as friends. In turn, your parents must learn to look upon you not just as their child, but as an individual who is capable of making independent decisions. Once you learn to see your parents as people, and they see you as an individual, you will be on your way to

becoming an adult – in charge of and responsible for your own actions.

Teen to Teen aims to help you develop your personal identity in a confident and safe way. On this journey of self-discovery, you will probably encounter many psychological, emotional, social, and physical challenges. This book offers information and guidance in subjects of the mind (academics and your professional future), body (puberty, body image, and sexual activity), and relationships (communication and values in friendship, romance, etc.) – so that as you develop, you can be informed, healthy, and proud of your individuality.

HANDLING EMOTIONS

Developing Self-Esteem

How would you describe the way you feel about yourself? Would you be more likely to describe yourself as confident, capable, and proud, or afraid, troubled, and insecure? You will probably feel different ways at different times. The thoughts and feelings you have about yourself, whether positive or negative, make up your self-esteem – a picture of how much you value yourself.

People who choose to describe themselves as "confident, capable, and proud" generally have high self-esteem. They think good thoughts about themselves and are able to recognize the positive aspects of what they do. Even when things go wrong, they can pick up the pieces and move on. Problems and failures become temporary setbacks – just learning experiences that help them keep going.

In contrast, people who choose to describe themselves as "afraid, troubled, and insecure" may have negative pictures of themselves and may have low self-esteem. Perhaps they continually blame themselves for things that go wrong even if it isn't their fault. It is difficult for them to feel good about themselves because they put themselves down. Or, they believe failures will prevent them from reaching their goals.

Few people have high self-esteem all the time. After all, everybody has doubts about themselves at one time or another. Fortunately, there are ways to get through these periods of low self-esteem.

Self-esteem is a learned way of thinking and feeling about yourself. These opinions are probably influenced by the opinions of your family, friends, teachers, and role models. Through their actions and attitudes, you get messages about what they think about you. Depending on what you take away from these messages, the words and gestures pass through your personal "filter" and you develop high or low self-esteem.

If someone calls you "ugly," you can choose how to react. Do you think, "I agree, I am ugly," or "That's not true, I know I'm attractive"? What do you think about the person who is making the comment? Do you respect that person's opinions? Is that person envious of you in some other area, or purposely trying to upset you? Does he or she simply want to get your attention, and is this an attempt at flirting? Always, before you let experiences change your opinion of yourself, analyze the situation and the people involved.

It's never too late to raise your self-esteem. Positive thoughts about yourself are often self-fulfilling. Once you start to feel good about yourself, you really do begin to look, act, and perform better than before.

Just as you are aware of your negative thoughts and how they can lead to low self-esteem, it is important to keep the positive thoughts in check, too. People with exceptionally high self-esteem might think that they are "perfect" and have trouble accepting criticism from others. This can lead to arrogance and difficulty dealing with people. It is great to feel good about yourself, but remember that we always have something to learn and appreciate from each other.

Setting Goals

High self-esteem usually means that a person thinks of him or herself as successful. Success can be whatever you want it to be – feeling confident, quitting smoking, getting a date, stopping drug use, going to the college of your choice, or finding a job. Setting goals that are worthy of you as a person is the single most important step in achieving success.

Most people have no problem imagining things they would like to have: a boyfriend, or girlfriend, a car, popularity, or money. But sometimes they either imagine too much all at once (so that their desires overwhelm them and they end up doing nothing), or they never actually take the step of changing their daydreams into goals. If you find you're having a problem turning your dreams into goals, consider some helpful steps to success:

1. **Put your dreams in writing.** This will be your long term goal. It may help to begin with words like "I intend," "I will," and "I plan." These three statements are more definite commitments to your dreams than "I wish," "I want," or "I don't want," or "I'll try."

2. **Break your goal into smaller steps that you can achieve.** Although your dreams can be as big and colorful as you want, it is important to set smaller, realistic target goals. Be specific! State an exact period of time to meet these goals. By today? By this week? By New Year's Day? Your overall goals can be as high as the sky, but thinking step-by-step is the most manageable way to reach your target. With each completed step, you will be reminded of your accomplishments and feel successful.

3. **Believe in yourself and your goals.** As long as you believe you can be successful, you will be able to take the next step. Draw upon past experiences and successes for guidance. How did you do it? What/who helped you in the past, and how can these same things/people help you now?

4. **Goals exist to serve you.** If you didn't achieve the result you intended, keep working at it. You haven't failed, but

you may need to take different steps toward your target goal. Remember to use the resources around you to help you achieve your goal.

••

Let's take Sabrina as an example of how to set goals:

Sabrina was oversleeping every day. It made her feel awful to have the whole morning be so rushed, and she and her mom usually got into a fight about it. Time and again, she said to herself, "I've just GOT to stop oversleeping." But the next day, she'd do it again, and feel guilty that she could not "get tough" with herself.

Sabrina sought help for her problem by talking to her older brother. Sabrina's brother asked her what she could do to help herself wake up on time. Sabrina suggested that she could buy herself an alarm clock and set it every night. The next week when her brother asked about it, Sabrina reported that she had gotten the clock and used it, but she'd turned over and gone back to sleep. Her brother then asked her what she could do to avoid turning over and going back to sleep. Sabrina thought about it and came up with the idea to place the clock across the room, so that she'd have to walk across the room to turn it off. Sabrina knew if she could get herself up on time just once in the next week, she would be on her way to achieving her goal.

••

All Sabrina's brother did was ask her questions that helped her break down her big desire ("I've got to stop oversleeping") into many small, manageable steps that she could do on her own. Each day, as Sabrina met a specific goal of getting up on time, she would feel more successful.

For many people, the best way to feel better about themselves is to make positive statements, or affirmations, about themselves. For example, here are some positive things you can say to yourself to help remember what a great person you are.

Affirmations (positive statements) for Today*

1. I am able to see problems as opportunities to be creative.
2. I am a success.
3. I am organized.
4. I am creative.
5. I am talented.
6. I love myself.
7. I discover the positive in most situations.
8. I take the time to listen to others.
9. I enjoy a job well done.
10. I start each day with joy and energy.
11. I am strong and healthy.
12. I am unique.
13. I am ready to take the next right step.

Here are some examples of negative or guilty thoughts that people have about themselves, and ways these thoughts can be changed into positive goals.

Guilt Trip		Positive Goal
I need to lose weight.	▶	I will lose 1 pound this week.
I should be doing better in school.	▶	I will pass each course this semester.
I've got to quit spending all my money on clothes.	▶	I'm going to save 10% of my next paycheck.
I've got to quit being so sloppy.	▶	This Saturday I will pick up .. and vacuum my room before going out.

Now you can do the same thing by writing out any negative thoughts or guilt trips on the left, and then re-writing them into positive goals on the right.

Adapted from "Affirmations," by Money and You – Management by Agreement, P.O. Box 55105, Atlanta, GA.

| **My Guilty Thoughts** | ► | **My Small Positive Goals** |

_____

_____

_____

_____

_____

_____

How to Be Successful: Barriers, Solutions, and People Who Can Help You with Your Plan

To help you be more successful at achieving your goals, it often helps to figure out what might get in your way so you can plan ahead for how you will deal with each barrier.

For example, Tina might be planning to quit smoking cigarettes by the end of this month. Some examples of barriers that she can come up with plan might be:
1. Getting stressed or upset and wanting to smoke since this is how Tina has always coped in the past.
2. Being with friends who are smoking and offer Tina a cigarette.

Some solutions to these two barriers could be:
1. Explore and learn new ways of coping with stress or feeling upset before it happens, so Tina doesn't need cigarettes to help her cope.
2. Plan in advance how she will deal with situations when friends offer her a cigarette, or come up with ways to avoid these types of situations.

It can also be useful to come up with a list of people who can help you with your plan and write down specifically what each person will do to help you. **Now you can do this with something you plan to do soon. List as many barriers as you can think of to your plan, and then prepare solutions for each barrier. Then list each person who you know can help you and what specifically each person will do to support you in your plan.** It can also be fun to do this with a friend, and see how many barriers and solutions you can come up with together.

My Success Plan will be to:

_____

_____

_____

_____

Some small steps I can take toward my goal are:

_____

_____

_____

_____

The reasons this is important to me are:

_____

_____

_____

_____

Some things that might get in the way of my plan are:

_____

_____

_____

_____

Some solutions to these barriers are:

_____

_____

_____

_____

People who can help me and what each person will do:

_____

_____

_____

_____

Depression

During the teenage years, as both your external (friends, school, jobs) and internal (body, feelings, sexuality) environments change, it is common to feel a little confused and "lost." Young people, noticing these changes, may begin to feel differently about themselves. They might question their place and value in the world: What am I good at? What do I want to do? Why am I changing like this? Where do I fit in? Who do I want to be? WHO AM I?

These questions and their answers constantly change, depending on how a person is feeling and what events a person is experiencing. As a result, it is normal for young people to have mood swings, so that sometimes they feel good and sometimes they feel bad. However, someone who feels deeply sad for a long period of time – usually more than a few weeks– may be experiencing depression. Depression is a mental health condition that describes long periods of low self-esteem, when a person feels worthless, hopeless, unmotivated, and generally unsatisfied with him or herself.

Mild depression can affect a person's behavior and performance in emotional, social, physical, and professional activities, while serious depression can make a person feel so hopeless and unhappy that he or she considers suicide. For these reasons, depression is very dangerous. Among 15-24 year olds in the United States, depression is the third leading cause of death, after motor vehicle accidents and homicide. In this age group in the U.S., there are 400,000 to 800,000 suicide attempts each year. Of these attempts, 4,000 (1 in 100 to 200) result in death.

For more information on identifying and dealing with depression, read on and visit the websites:

http://kidshealth.org/teen/your_mind

http://www.helpguide.org/mental/depression_teen.htm.

Or you can call The National Mental Health Association at 1-800-969-6642 or a National Suicide Hotline for teens like 1-800-SUICIDE or 1-800-784-2433.

What causes depression?
There is no one answer to this question, because everybody can feel depressed for different reasons. Some types of depression are from a chemical imbalance, while other types are a reaction to a difficult or stressful situation. Often it is an unhappy event, confusion, or failure that triggers depression. Some people can feel depressed when they do badly at school, while others might be unhappy when they fight with their parents, question their family's religious beliefs, or read horrible news in the paper. Although everyone faces challenges and disappointments, and will sometimes feel unhappy, how you handle depression depends on your self-esteem and how you deal with problems.

How does depression feel, from the inside?
Depression is a deep sadness that people can experience for a long period of time – from several days to an entire lifetime. It can make you feel tired, bored, irritable, useless, aimless, unworthy, confused, or just empty. Sometimes with depression, a person might have persistent negative thoughts about themselves. On some mornings, it might be difficult to get out of bed because there doesn't seem to be anything worth while to do; at night, it might be difficult to fall asleep because you feel lonely, unhappy, and unsatisfied with the day's events. Some say that depression feels like a cloud hanging over your head, creating a spot of darkness and sogginess that you feel you cannot escape. According to the University of Iowa Health Care, just over 8% of adolescents are actually diagnosed with depression. However, even adolescents who have not been diagnosed with depression commonly feel depressed in response to unfortunate events, disappointing news, or scary experiences.

What does depression look like, from the outside?
When a person is depressed and feels bad about him or herself, he or she might display external signs of this internal negativity. There are several changes in behavior and appearance including

activities that show a lack of concern for one's own well-being that might be signs of depression. They include:
- oversleeping
- difficulty sleeping
- overeating
- difficulty eating
- poor hygiene (no showers or lack of concern about appearance)
- doing dangerous activities
- poor attendance at school and other activities
- poor performance in school and other activities
- lack of focus or enthusiasm, where there used to be some
- using drugs or alcohol
- avoiding social situations with family and friends

What can I do about depression?
Be on the lookout for depression in yourself and your friends, but remember that the above behaviors can only point toward depression – a person acting this way is not necessarily depressed. Before you jump to conclusions about a friend's self-esteem and mental health state, talk with him or her about these feelings. If you think you might be depressed, you can also talk to friends, parents, teachers, counselors, and health care providers about your mood or concerns about a friend's mood. Talking about problems can release a lot of negative energy, and simply knowing that someone is listening can lift a great weight off of a person's shoulders. It is important to know that your friends, family, and mentors are there for support, so that no one battles alone against depression.

Will it ever end?
Those who experience depression often say that it is a lifelong battle, as the mental illness can disappear and reappear many times over the years. However, millions of Americans live with depression and still have balanced, successful, happy lives. They might take medications like Prozac, Zoloft, Celexa, Lexapro, Paxil, or Luvox which increase levels of serotonin, a chemical in the brain associated with good moods, to help control their emotions. Teenagers can take these drugs safely but only if they are closely monitored by a health care provider to make sure that they do not become suicidal. Other popular therapies for

depression include counseling with a therapist or psychiatrist, physical activities like yoga and running, companionship with other people and pets, and satisfying paid or volunteer work. Some of these therapies may work for you or someone you know, and there are many other activities that can also help. Simply having a meaningful project to do – like tending a garden or writing a book – can make a person feel much better, so explore the possibilities and find something that makes you feel good!

If you need help finding ways to live with depression, visit the website: http://www.mental-health-matters.com/crisis/800numb.php for references to helpful information and counseling services.

Loneliness
••

Being far from home and alone

At 17, I moved away from home and tried to pretend I understood how to survive on my own. I tried to work to pay the rent, pursue my dance career, and have relationships with people who were older than me. This was one of the loneliest times of my life.

••

Everyone goes through periods of loneliness. Loneliness is an emotion that is felt by different people in different ways. Lots of people, like the young woman who moved away, get lonely when they have no friends their age and are alone in a new place. Some people feel particularly lonely when their friends all have boyfriends and girlfriends, and they don't. Other people feel very lonely when their parents fight with each other. Loneliness is a part of the journey through life.

Eventually, we all develop ways to help ourselves get through the lonely times – it's just part of growing up. Here is how some young people deal with loneliness:

My loneliness is helped by...
    ...crying
    ...dancing
    ...praying
    ...listening to music
    ...playing sports (alone like running, or with a team)
    ...writing
    ...painting
    ...talking to parents/friends
    ...walking the dog
    ...helping someone else

Feeling alone and lonely at times is normal, but it does not mean that you should feel bad about yourself. Healthy loneliness is a sad feeling about the situation; unhealthy loneliness develops when your sad feelings are focused on yourself. If you notice yourself or a friend dealing with loneliness in an unhealthy way, talk about it and work on positive methods of coping. Some warning signs of unhealthy loneliness include:

- withdrawal from conversation, group activity, and social scenes
- excessive crying
- self put-downs (insulting oneself) or having persistent negative thoughts about yourself
- cutting and other forms of self-mutilation or injury

Many symptoms of unhealthy loneliness look like the warning signs for depression. That's because the two states are closely related, and one can often affect or lead to the other. Once again, be on the lookout for yourself and your friends!

It takes time to learn what is the best way for YOU to combat loneliness. Once you learn a healthy approach to loneliness, remember it and use it the next time. Keep in mind that everyone experiences loneliness at some point or another, and even if you feel bad, healthy coping behaviors will help you overcome the situation.

Coping with Stress

••

Stephanie's boyfriend wants her to have sex with him, but that's not what she wants.

Eric has a big test tomorrow, and he hasn't studied yet.

Byron and his best friend, Will, are competing for the same position on the basketball team. The last day of try-outs is this afternoon.

Tanesha had another huge fight with her parents last night. She doesn't want to get angry at them, but she feels they don't listen to her.

••

What do all these situations have in common? They show people in stressful situations. Though sometimes stress can be positive, most people think of stress as a physical, mental, or emotional strain. One thing is for sure – stress is a constant part of life. How people handle stress has a lot to do with how they stay healthy.

Exploring your sexuality can be especially stressful because everything seems to be changing so quickly. Your body is changing, you may be developing stronger sexual feelings or attractions to different people, you might be starting to have serious relationships, and you may suddenly feel pressured to have sexual intercourse.

There are lots of ways to recognize stress when it happens to you. Below are some signals of stress, some of which will surely sound familiar. Stress signals* include:

Adapted Kate Rafferty and Mary Jo Herde, Help Yourself! *(New Hampshire Department of Education, 1980); reprinted in the Education Development Center's publication* Handling Stress.

Physical
- increased heart rate – pounding and palpitations
- sweaty palms and feet
- headaches
- tight or cramped muscles
- trembling, twitching, or shaking
- stuttering
- nausea and/or vomiting
- difficulty sleeping, tiredness
- being accident prone
- nervous laughter
- frequent minor illnesses
- dry mouth or throat

Emotional
- irritability, angry outbursts
- lowered self-esteem, depression, withdrawal
- suspiciousness, restlessness
- crying easily
- self-criticism

Mental
- forgetfulness
- nightmares
- decreased or increased fantasy life
- less creativity, less productivity
- difficulty concentrating
- not paying attention to details
- thinking constantly about the past

Behavioral
- smoking
- reckless (risky) driving
- alcohol or drug use
- withdrawal from others
- carelessness

Recognizing signals of stress is a real help in learning to cope with it. If you can tell that you're just angry at your best friend because you are worried about a test, you can stop yourself from saying something to your friend that you might regret. You can also take steps to decrease your stress.

People cope with stress in many different ways. There is no single right way to handle stress. Each of us needs to decide what is best for ourselves. Lots of people find that physical activity or exercise is a great stress reliever. Many people turn to their religious beliefs for comfort. Other people may just need to forget about their problems for a while by watching T.V. or going to a movie. For some, the best thing to do when they are overwhelmed with things to do is to make a list of what they need to do and when they want to get it done. This way, they can see that it is possible to finish everything. Last, many people take time out of their hectic lives to let themselves relax. This can be done by finding some time for yourself. Lie down, take several very deep breaths, and let the tension flow out of your body. You may be surprised by how well a daily relaxation exercise can work. **Here is an example of a relaxation exercise you can do:**

Relaxation Imagery Exercise*
Prepare
Find a quiet, comfortable place to sit.
Take one or two or three slow, deep, comforting breaths
And clear your mind.
Part 1
Press your index finger & thumb firmly together...
While you take a deep breath in and hold it....
And close your eyes (to shut out outside visual distractions)...
Hold this breath and finger press for a slow count to 5...
Part 2
At the count of 5, let the breath out...
Let the finger pressure go...
Keep the eyes closed...
Notice the relaxation beginning...

Now, Take 5... slow... deep... breaths... in... and ...out...   On each breath out... Let the relaxation spread.... more and more... so that by the 5th breath out... you can be as relaxed... and as comfortable....as you want.

---

*Adapted from Daniel P. Kohen, M.D., Department of Pediatrics, University of Minnesota (personal communication)

As you do this and feel good, pay attention to the tension that goes away...and to the way that you do that... and notice what imaginary special place comes to mind... that you might be visiting in your mind's eye....

Let your mind linger in your favorite place and notice everything about it...the way it looks...the way it sounds... the way it smells, feels, and tastes...

Enjoy your relaxation for as long as you want...

When you are finished, you can re-orient yourself to where you started by slowly opening your eyes, and bringing your relaxation with you for as long as you need it.

It is good to remember that with each practice, this exercise becomes easier, more automatic, and more relaxing.

Here are 3 simple things you can say to yourself to decrease stress when you begin to feel under pressure:
　　1. **Don't sweat the little things.**
　　2. **Most things are little things.**
　　3. **If I can't fight it or run from it, I'll go with the flow.**

These are not the only ways to cope with stress; they are just some suggestions that have worked for other people. The key to coping with the stress, in the end, is to recognize that you are stressed out and to find the best way for you to handle it. Stress is a natural part of life, and it happens to all of us – it's just part of being human.

To help you be more aware of your own stress signals, see how you can fill out the lines below:

How I know when I am stressed:

_____

_____

_____

Situations that make me feel this way:

_____

_____

_____

Things I can do to decrease my stress:

_____

_____

_____

Bullying and Cyberbullying

What is bullying? Bullying is a form of abuse that can happen in school or other social settings. Bullying can come from one person or a group of people who are being cruel to another person. There are different types of bullying such as physical abuse including pushing, shoving, hitting, or forcing someone to do something they don't want to do. Bullies can also threaten, taunt, spread rumors (gossip), or say hurtful things. This is called verbal abuse. There is also nonverbal or emotional bullying, which can include intimidating someone through gestures or excluding them socially. More recently, people use their computers and cellular phones to bully and harass. This is called cyberbullying. With cyberbullying, the teasing and harassment can carry on long after the school bell rings to mark the end of the day.

Some examples of cyberbullying include:
- Sending or posting hateful, cruel or threatening text or images using the Internet or other digital communication devices
- Creating web sites that have rumors, stories, cartoons, pictures, and jokes ridiculing others
- Posting pictures of people online and asking others to rate them, with questions like "Who is the biggest .....?"

- Hacking into another person's e-mail account and sending mean or embarrassing material to others that make the emails appear to be coming from the person who is being bullied.
- Getting someone to respond to IM (instant messaging) and tricking that person into sharing sensitive personal information, and then forwarding that information to others
- Taking a picture of a person undressing in a locker room or using the restroom using a digital phone camera, and sending that picture to others to embarrass that person

How often does bullying happen? It is more common than you might think. In studies, 15 to 25 percent of U.S. students say they are bullied "sometimes or more often" while 15 to 20 percent of students say they bully others with some frequency. Boys are more likely than girls to bully others but girls can be bullies too. Girls frequently report being bullied by both boys and girls, but boys most often report being bullied only by other boys.
What are the consequences of bullying? Young people who bully are more likely than those who do not bully to skip classes and drop out of school. They are also more likely to smoke cigarettes, drink alcohol and get into fights. People who use computers or cell phones to bully others often think it is a way to harass others while keeping their identities hidden. This is not true. Instant messaging, emails and other computer communication activities can always be traced. It is a serious matter. All forms of bullying, especially cyberbullying, can lead to criminal charges, lawsuits, loss of computer privileges, suspension or expulsion from school, and other serious consequences.

Another serious aspect of bullying is the severe physical and psychological damage to the person being bullied. Teens who are bullied are more likely than others to be depressed, lonely, anxious; have low self-esteem, feel unwell, and think about suicide.

What can you do? If you or someone you know is being bullied, you NEED to take action and not ignore it. There are several things you can do to stop bullying. The most important thing to realize is that it is not your fault if you are being bullied. People bully others because they often feel scared or powerless themselves and have low self-esteem. They hurt others to help themselves feel stronger and more powerful. Bullying is not personal. It is not about you. Instead, it is about a feeling of control that the bully has as he or she hurts people. If you are the target of bullying, there is nothing wrong with you as a person.

If bullying is ignored, it will not go away. By taking effective and nonviolent action against bullying you will protect yourself and ensure that the bully stops. As a result, you and others will not be in fear of being bullied any longer! If you feel you are a victim of bullying or if you see someone else is a victim of bullying you should do the following:

Talk your parents or an adult you trust IMMEDIATELY. Your parents, teachers and school officials want to keep you safe. It is important to let them know that there is a problem, so they can help you. Explain to them exactly what is happening and who is bullying you. If you see someone else being bullied, report it to an adult as soon as possible. It is often easier for a person who witnesses bullying to report it to an adult than it is for the person being bullied to report it. Writing down what has happened, when it happened, and who was there will help you to report a bullying incident. If you are reporting cyberbullying, save any emails, instant and text messages, blogs, and websites so you have proof of what has been going on. Do not use the computer to "fight back".

Providing adults with detailed information about bullying will help them to confront the bullies about their unacceptable behavior. It is important for someone to tell the bully that what he or she is doing is not acceptable behavior and that serious consequences will follow if the behavior continues. This feedback is often most effective coming from an adult or someone of authority.

Stay in a group. If you feel threatened at school or in social situations where a bully might be present, stay in a group. If possible, avoid being alone when using the restroom, going into empty rooms or walking the halls. Bullies are less likely to target you if you are in a group and other students can be supportive to you in a stressful situation. Other people can also be witnesses to the bully's actions. Generally, a bully is less likely to target you when he or she knows they could easily be caught and punished for their actions.

The best thing you can do for a person who is being bullied is to be supportive and understanding. For example, you can agree to go to the rest room with them, walk home with them after school, and include them in your school or social activities. This may not sound like a lot, but it can really help someone who is being bullied!

Stand up to the person who is bullying you. Confronting bullies on your own can be stressful and challenging. However, standing up to bullies tells them know that their behavior will not be tolerated. If you feel comfortable talking to a bully, be calm and do not get into a fight. It is better not to try to reason with or convince a bully to stop harassing you. Tell him or her that you don't like the way you are being treated, that what they are doing is wrong, and that it needs to stop. If you think that talking to a bully is not helpful, walk away. This is a mature and peaceful approach, and is better than using angry words or physical violence. If you see someone else being bullied, tell the bully to stop. Even better, get some friends to join you (there is power in numbers!) It may not be easy to stand up to a bully who is bigger and stronger, or more popular than you, but it works! Just be sure you do not fall into the trap of bullying them back.

Make a joke. It can be hard to make a joke in a serious situation, but humor can help! Bullies prefer to pick on people who get upset easily. If someone is picking on you and you joke about it, you'll show them you cannot be easily upset and chances are they will stop or go target someone else.

Some websites on bullying and how to deal with it include:
http://www.ncvc.org
http://www.safeyouth.org
http://www.cyberbully.org
http://i-safe.org
http://www.stopbullyingnow.hrsa.gov

CHANGING BODIES

Have you noticed that some of the people you know look different than they used to? Some guys and some girls look much older, more mature, …more like adults. You may also have noticed these changes in yourself. Such changes in your body mean that you are going through (or have gone through) puberty. This is part of becoming a young adult. Many of the changes in the way you act and the way you think about yourself, discussed in previous chapters, are greatly affected by your physical maturity and how comfortable you are with your new body.

How does your body change during puberty? The beginning of puberty happens at various times, usually between ages 9-17 years. There is no "magic age" at which all teenagers reach puberty. It may depend on your genes, the pattern inherited from your family. The physical changes that happen during puberty will continue for several years until your body reaches its mature shape. Some of the common changes for both males and females are growth of underarm and pubic hair, and growth spurts. Even though puberty can be an uncomfortable and challenging period of your life, it is also very exciting. Remember that your physical and emotional changes are probably normal, and that most other people have had similar experiences and can relate to yours.

Keep in mind that puberty may begin at different ages for males and females. There is no need to feel ashamed if you feel you are developing earlier or later than most other people around you. Eventually everyone reaches physical maturity. Also, it can help to remember that you may not be the only one of your peers in this situation. Others around you may be having the same thoughts and feelings about their puberty. You can learn to accept your body as it is changing, and to appreciate its uniqueness.

How do you know if delayed puberty is a medical problem?
Puberty may begin at different ages for boys and for girls. However, if you are a girl and do not start breast development by age 13 or get your period by age 16, you should tell your doctor or nurse. For a girl who has been having monthly periods, if your period doesn't come for more than 2 or 3 cycles in a row, you

should get this checked out too. For boys, if your testicles do not start growing by age 13 or if you do not develop pubic hair by 14 or 15, tell your doctor or nurse.

More information on growth and development is available at:

http://www.teenhealthtalk.org

General information on puberty can be found at:

http://kidshealth.org/teen/sexual_health

http://www.iwannaknow.org/puberty/index.html

Male Development

During puberty, guys have physical changes such as deepening of the voice, broadening of the shoulders, growing facial and body hair, and the penis gets wider and longer. Because everyone is different, how much and how fast your body changes compared to your friends will be different. The male sex hormone that causes these changes is testosterone and it is made by the testicles. One of the things testosterone does is to tell the testicles to make sperm.

Sperm are the half that a guy gives to create a baby. When a male's sperm join with a female's egg, the egg is fertilized. However, sperm need a way to get to the woman's egg, if the egg is to be fertilized. Sperm travel in a white, sticky fluid called semen. The prostate gland, located just below the bladder, produces over 90% of the male's semen. Sperm are very sensitive to heat, and they must be kept several degrees cooler than the body temperature in order to survive. Because of this temperature requirement, a boy's testicles hang down and away from his body (and body heat). If a guy is swimming in cold water, his testicles will actually pull in closer to his body for more warmth.

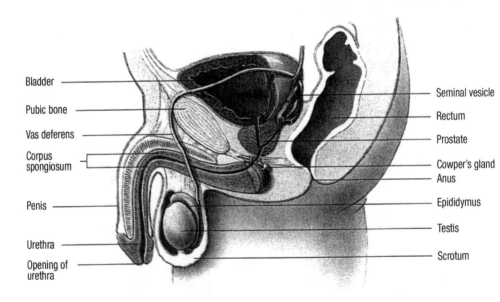

Bladder

Pubic bone

Vas deferens

Corpus spongiosum

Penis

Urethra

Opening of urethra

Seminal vesicle

Rectum

Prostate

Cowper's gland

Anus

Epididymus

Testis

Scrotum

A guy has an erection, or "hard-on," when sexual excitement causes blood to flow into his penis, causing the penis to swell. If sexual excitement continues, he may ejaculate (cum), releasing the semen that was made in the prostate gland. The semen travels from the prostate gland through a tube called the vas deferens, and is released through another tube called the urethra (the same place where urine is released). Each ejaculate has 100 to 400 million sperm. Guys can also get erections when they are anxious or even with temperature changes.

Managing Your Body and Health
Erections can happen when they are not expected, and sometimes guys can feel embarrassed about them, especially when they happen in social situations like at school or in front of adults or friends. In addition to being sexually excited when you are awake, during the night you may have fantasies which lead to erections and ejaculation. When guys wake up with wet bed sheets, it is often called a "wet dream." If you experience a wet dream, don't worry; this is a sign of normal development. You shouldn't be embarrassed about having a healthy sex drive, although sometimes wet dreams come when they are least expected. If you haven't had any "wet dreams" yet, that is also normal.

Another thing that often happens to guys as they are going through puberty is that one or both areas of the chest under the nipples will get tender or sore and grow. This does not mean you are developing breasts! It is a common condition called gynecomastia (guy – neh – co – MAST – ee – ah) and it is normal. As your hormones are changing during puberty, a slight imbalance of female hormones can cause the tissue under the nipples to get tender and grow. This can happens to almost two-thirds of guys but it usually goes away on it's own in about 6 months. If you have gynecomastia lasting longer than 6 to 9 months, tell your health care provider.

The Male Genital Exam
A male genital exam is advised for guys who are 9 years or older. Some of the many reasons for getting a male genital exam include:

- wanting to find out if everything is normal
- no pubic hair development or enlargement of the testicles or penis by age 14
- discharge from the penis, or sores or bumps on the penis or scrotum
- fear of sexually transmitted infection (see STD section, page 143)
- scrotal or testicular pain or a mass or lump

Why is the male genital exam so important?

The male genital exam is one of the most important routine medical exams for men to have. During the exam, you can discuss specific concerns about your penis, testicles and scrotum. You can also ask for advice about ways to help your female partner prevent pregnancy and help yourself prevent sexually transmitted diseases. Male genital exams are also important because they allow your health care provider to find and treat many types of sexually transmitted diseases.

What happens during the male genital exam?

The male genital exam includes several steps. First, a counselor, doctor, or nurse takes your medical history, focusing on the reason for the exam and gathering information about your sexual history. This may seem like prying, but these are important things for your health care provider to know to make sure you are healthy. Your health care provider should keep all your health information confidential (meaning private) and should not share it with anyone (including your parents) without your permission. The only time a health care provider might need to breach your confidentiality (tell information without your permission) is if you are homicidal (going to kill another person), suicidal (going to kill yourself) or if you are under the age of 18 and you report that you are being physically or sexually abused. However, you can always refuse to give information.

After taking your medical history, your health care provider will feel your abdomen and the lymph nodes in your groin, and look at the external genitalia (pubic hair, penis, urethral opening, and scrotum). Your health care provider will be looking for any discharge from the opening of the penis (urethral opening), and will check the penis and scrotum for any lumps, bumps or sores. The health care provider will also do a testicular exam where he or she will roll each testicle between the thumb and fingers to feel for any lumps or bumps that could be a sign of testicular cancer. You may also be shown how to do a self-testicular exam (see below).

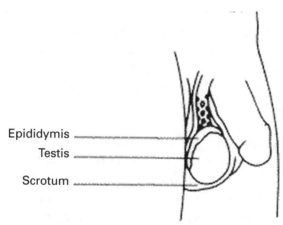

Epididymis
Testis
Scrotum

The health care provider will also slowly insert a gloved finger into the loose skin of the scrotum and push upward to feel your inguinal canal. This is done to check for a hernia (a hole in the inner wall of the abdomen that allows the intestines to move into the scrotum.) You may be asked to turn your head to one side and cough or bear down like you are having a bowel movement and then you will be asked to turn your head to the other side and do the same thing again.

Sometimes your health care provider may also recommend a rectal exam, particularly if you have anal intercourse or have any rectal complaints or abdominal pain. During this part of the exam, your health care provider will place one lubricated gloved finger into your rectum. Your health care provider will feel your rectal canal for lumps or masses and check for any changes in the normal smoothness of your prostate gland. Although rectal exams may seem a little frightening at first, they can answer important questions you have about your body and reproductive health. You can help the exam feel more comfortable by taking slow, deep breaths into your abdomen.

What if you get an erection when the health care provider is examining you? This is perfectly normal and you should not feel embarrassed about it. Your health care provider will know that this is normal and that is does not mean you are having sexual feelings at the time of the genital exam. Having an erection during a genital exam does not mean anything about your sexuality. Many men get erections when being examined by male doctors and this does not mean they are sexually attracted to men. However, if you feel more comfortable being examined by a female or a male health care provider, it is a good idea to let your health care provider's office know at the time you schedule your appointment so they can meet your request.

As your body develops, the risk of testicular cancer also increases slightly. Although testicular cancer is fairly rare, it is one of the most common cancers that affect young men. Testicular cancer can be cured if caught early. It is important to learn from your doctor or nurse how to do a testicular self exam correctly. Here are some general instructions on how to do it:

How to Do a Testicular Self-Examination
It is best to examine yourself once a month. If you check too frequently, like every day, you can't tell if anything is changing. The best place to check is in the shower or bath because the warm, soapy water allows your testicles to hang down and roll more easily. Using your thumb, index and middle fingers, roll each testicle, one at a time, feeling the entire surface. The testicle should feel smooth and rubbery like a hard-boiled egg without the shell on it. There should be no lumps or bumps. You can also feel the tubing that comes out of the testicle (called the vas deferens or spermatic cord) for lumps and tenderness. The vas deferens runs up the scrotum (the skin sac that holds the testicles) into the groin. If you ever notice a lump in the scrotum or on a testicle, or if you develop pain in a testicle or the vas deferens, seek medical attention as soon as possible.

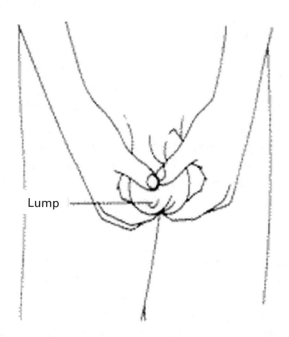

Lump

For more information, you can also check out the website at:

http://kidshealth.org/teen/sexual_health/guys/tse.html

Monthly exams can help you find and get treatment for early forms of testicular cancer.

Female Development

As girls go through puberty, they experience breast and pubic hair growth, a widening of the hips, and an increase in fat in the abdominal and hip areas. Once again, remember that everybody is different. You may have smaller or larger breasts than your friends; they may have different body shapes than you. Your breasts may not be exactly the same size. There are many shapes and sizes that are all normal. However, if you have concerns about the way you are growing, ask your doctor or nurse.

The Female Reproductive System

The main hormone that causes the physical changes of puberty in girls is estrogen. Estrogen from the ovaries and other hormones from the brain rise and fall in cycles that cause ovulation (the release of an egg) and menstruation (the shedding of the uterine lining, the egg's "bed," in the form of bleeding). When this cycling happens, you will start to have monthly periods. It can take several months to 2 years to get regular, monthly periods.

Ovulation is the release of an egg from the ovaries; usually, only one egg is released per cycle. Once you start to ovulate, you can get pregnant. With each egg, it is possible to get pregnant if sperm come close to the egg. Be aware that you can get pregnant before having your first period, since you don't know when your first ovulation will occur.

Before you ovulate, estrogen causes the lining of the uterus to thicken and prepare for a fertilized egg to grow there. If the egg is not fertilized by a sperm and you do not get pregnant, menstruation (the bleeding in your period) occurs as the lining of the uterus sheds. This lining is made of surface cells from the lining of the uterus and blood, which is why menstruation is often called "bleeding."

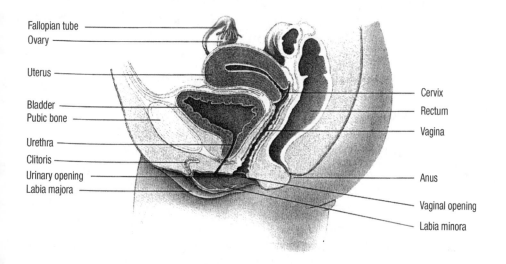

Fallopian tube
Ovary
Uterus
Bladder
Pubic bone
Urethra
Clitoris
Urinary opening
Labia majora

Cervix
Rectum
Vagina
Anus
Vaginal opening
Labia minora

A menstrual cycle is the period of time from the start of one bleeding period to the start of the next; the average cycle length is 28 days. For some women the cycle is shorter (21-25 days), and for others it may be longer (30-40 days). Twenty percent of women never have regular bleeding cycles. Your period may last from 2 to 7 days, and the blood flow may be light, moderate, or heavy. Each woman has different experiences when her period comes. Some are excited by their first period, but others are frightened by the experience. Being prepared and learning what to expect can help you feel good about this normal part of female development.

It is normal to have some vaginal discharge during your menstrual cycle. Often, after a period is over, there may be little or no discharge. As you go through the first 2 weeks of the cycle, you may have a clear or white stringy or mucus-like discharge. After ovulation, the discharge often becomes white and pasty for a week or so. This is usually followed by menstrual bleeding.

If your menstrual period lasts longer than 8 days, is very heavy, crampy or concerns you in any way, you may want to talk to your doctor or nurse. He or she can often tell you what you can do to make your periods less bothersome, and can make sure there are no health problems causing your period complaints.

Managing Menstruation
Women may use tampons, maxi pads, or both to collect the blood flow of their periods. You can use tampons even if you have never had sex. It is better to use unscented tampons or pads because the perfume used in the scented kind may irritate your skin. Many women like to use a tampon because it makes them more comfortable than a pad. However, you should not leave a tampon inside your vagina for longer than eight hours because this can increase your risk for a potentially serious infection called Toxic Shock Syndrome (TSS). All companies that make tampons give written information on TSS and directions for using their products, so check out a tampon box at the grocery store if you're curious! More information on menstrual protection can be found at:
http://www.youngwomenshealth.org/menstrual6.html

It is helpful to pay attention to your own menstrual pattern, which includes start and stop dates, the heaviness of the flow, and any symptoms you have before or during your period (cramps, bloating, back pain, nausea, diarrhea, or breast tenderness). Using a calendar to keep track of the days of your bleeding can help you learn your cycle and better answer questions that doctors and nurses might have about your period.

You may notice natural signs that signal when your period is about to start, such as fullness in the abdomen, constipation or diarrhea, backaches, headaches, or breast tenderness. But even when you pay attention to your cycle, your period can sometimes surprise you... It is a good idea to carry extra tampons or pads with you, even if you do not expect you will be bleeding.

You may wonder if your period is normal. Here are some questions you may ask yourself. If you answer "yes" to one or more of these questions, you may want to talk to a health care provider for help.

1. Do you bleed for more than 7 days?
2. Has your flow of menstrual blood greatly increased or decreased since you started menstruating? Since beginning or changing birth control methods?
3. Do you soak more than five sanitary napkins (pads) or tampons a day during your period?
4. Do you have a period more than every 4 weeks? Do you have a period less than once every 6 weeks?
5. Do you have spotting of blood (light bleeding) between regular periods?
6. Are your menstrual cramps or other menstrual- related complaints so severe that they keep you from your daily activities (like going to school or work or doing activities you like to do)?
7. Do you get menstrual cramps or pain that is so bad that they do not get better with over-the-counter pain medicine, exercise, or some other home remedy?
8. Do you get severe mood changes (depression, crying, unhappiness, nervousness) or headaches around the time of your period?

Premenstrual Symptoms (PMS) and Cramps

Premenstrual problems and menstrual cramping are common problems for teenagers and older women alike. Each year, U.S. women lose about 140 million hours from school or work because of severe menstrual cramps or pain. Sixty percent of young women aged 12-17 have some cramps and for more than 1 out of 10 of these women, these cramps are severe. However, most women don't have many problems with their periods.

Prostaglandin inhibitors such as ibuprofen (Motrin®, Advil®, and Nuprin®) and naproxen sodium (Aleve) are available over the counter, while Anaprox® is available by prescription. They all can decrease menstrual pain and cramps. For best results with ibuprofen, take 600 mg (3 over-the-counter tablets) with food every 6 hours, starting the day before your period. When using Aleve® or naproxen sodium, start with 2 tablets and then decrease to one tablet every 6 to 8 hours with food. Many hormonal birth control methods, like birth control pills, Depo-Provera® shots, the contraceptive patch, and the vaginal ring, can also help reduce menstrual cramps.

Some other home remedies that women find helpful are: using a heating pad or the new over-the-counter single use ThermaCare™ Heat Wraps that stay warm for 8 hours; doing vigorous exercise such as running; massaging the lower back, leg, or calf; lying with knees to the chest (while lying on the side or back); drinking hot liquids; resting; taking a warm bath, shower, or sauna; and cutting back on salt and increasing the amount of water you drink. Taking a calcium supplement and making sure you get 1300 mg of calcium a day can also help with PMS.

Girls may notice increased sexual arousal during puberty and before menstruation. When sexually aroused, girls may have increased wetness (lubrication) coming from the vagina.

Douching, Shaving, and Vaginal Hygiene
When you go to the grocery store or pharmacy and walk along the feminine hygiene product aisle, you may see lots of products that claim to make you smell "fresh as a meadow." In general, feminine washes, sprays, and powders are not only unnecessary, but they can also irritate your skin. If you have an odor or smell that does not seem right to you, it is best to get this checked out by your doctor or nurse rather than trying to cover it up with a perfumed product.

You may also see advertisements for douches. Douching is when a women rinses out the vagina with a liquid. Over 50 years ago, it was believed this was a good way to keep the vagina clean. But now we know better! When you rinse out the vagina with a douche, you wash out normal fluids and healthy bacteria that protect your vagina from unhealthy bacteria. This can allow an overgrowth of a bacteria infection of the vagina called Bacterial Vaginosis (BV). For more information on BV, see page 157.

So how should you keep your vagina clean? Just use a mild cleanser like unscented Dove® on a soft washcloth, plus plenty of water in the bath or shower. When bathing, use your fingers to separate the folds of the vagina and wipe away any dried discharge. Then rinse thoroughly, since soap residue can irritate your vagina and cause burning, itching, and redness. Avoid using heavily perfumed, deodorant, and liquid soaps as well as bubble bath products around the vagina, as these can be harder to rinse off completely.

What about shaving? It is completely natural to allow your pubic and armpit hair to grow. But some girls prefer to remove some or all of this body hair. Armpit and pubic area hair can be removed with chemical depilatories (products you put on the hair to dissolve it like Nair®) but these products can cause skin irritation for people with sensitive skin, and they have an unpleasant smell. Others prefer to remove hair by shaving with a razor. If you plan to shave, here are a few tips:
1. Do not share razors – sharing razors can pass infections like HIV and Hepatitis B and C.
2. Do not leave your razor in the bath or shower – because of the moisture, the blade will get rusty and bacteria may grow on it.
3. Shave in the direction of the hair, not against it – you may not get as close of a shave but you will be less likely to yank hairs and get folliculitis (an infection at the base of the hair).
4. Use a lot of moisturizing soap, lubricating gel, or shaving cream – this may prevent razor burn.

Finally, some prefer to remove hair by body waxing, either at home or professionally. This can be painful, expensive and time-consuming, but it is less likely than shaving to cause skin infections. Also, waxing removes the hair for a longer period of time than shaving. Because home waxing kits are extremely hot and can burn your skin, it may be a better idea to get your waxing done professionally.

The Pelvic Exam
A pelvic exam is advised for women who are 21 years or older, or younger than 21 years and sexually active or for anyone who has been sexually molested. Some of the many reasons for getting a pelvic exam include:
• wanting to find out if everything is normal

- painful menstrual periods that have not improved with over the counter or prescription medications
- no period by age 14 in a young women who have not developed breasts or pubic hair
- no period by age 16 even if growth and development of breasts and pubic hair have been normal
- severe pelvic pain
- known or suspected rape or sexual abuse
- bothersome vaginal discharge or fear of sexually transmitted infection (see STD section, page 143)
- unexplained abdominal pain or a pelvic mass
- possibility of pregnancy

If you want to start a prescription birth control method like the pill, the patch, the ring, or the shot AND you have never had penis-in-vagina sex, you do not have to get a pelvic exam before starting it. However, if you have ever had sex, your doctor or nurse might recommend a pelvic exam to check for sexually transmitted diseases and cervical cancer.

Why is the pelvic exam so important?
The pelvic exam is one of the most important routine medical exams for women to have. During the exam, you can discuss specific menstrual problems, and ask for advice about safe and effective birth control methods. Pelvic exams are also important because they allow your health care provider to find and treat many types of sexually transmitted diseases, especially those that might cause you to have problems having babies later on.

What happens during the pelvic exam?
The pelvic exam includes several steps. First, a counselor, doctor, or nurse takes your medical history, focusing on the reason for the exam and gathering information about your sexual history. This may seem like prying, but these are important things for your health care provider to know to make sure you are healthy. Your health care provider should keep all your health information confidential (meaning private) and should not share it with anyone (including your parents) without your permission. The only time a health care provider might need to breach your confidentiality (tell information without your permission) is if you

are homicidal (going to kill another person), suicidal (going to kill yourself) or if you are under the age of 18 and you report that you are being physically or sexually abused. However, you can always refuse to give information.

After taking your medical history, your health care provider will feel your armpits and your breasts, feeling for unusual lumps or masses under the skin. Ask your health care provider to show you how to examine your own breasts. Monthly breast self-examinations can help you learn what is normal for you now and help you find early forms of breast cancer when you get older so it can be treated early and cured.

Next, your health care provider will feel your abdomen and the lymph nodes in your groin, and look at the external genitalia (pubic hair

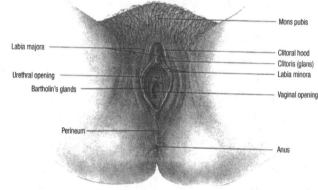

The health care provider will slowly insert a small warmed speculum into your vagina and then open it gently to see the walls of the vagina and the cervix. A speculum is an instrument to hold open the walls of the vagina made of metal or plastic. When a speculum is put in, it often feels like something sliding into the vagina like a tampon applicator or a finger.

You can help the exam feel more comfortable by taking slow, deep breaths into your abdomen and by pressing your hips down into the table as you let your legs flop open at the knees. During the speculum exam, your health care provider looks at your

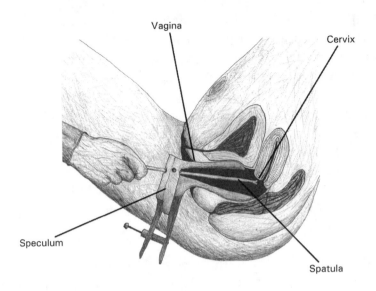

Vagina

Cervix

Speculum

Spatula

cervix and the walls of your vagina.

If you have ever had penis-in-vagina sex, your health care provider will test for sexually transmitted diseases like gonorrhea and chlamydia and give you information about preventing these infections. Your health care provider may also gently rub off cells from your cervix with a soft brush and a spatula to do a Pap smear test, which checks for cervical cancer.

Your health care provider may also collect some discharge from the vagina with a cotton swab to look for other infections (like yeast, bacterial vaginosis (BV), and trichomonas) under a microscope and check the pH balance of the wall of the vagina with a pH strip to see how acidic or basic it is. The vagina should normally have a pH balance of 4.5 or less. If the pH balance is too high, it might mean you have an infection like trichomonas or BV (although semen in the vagina can make the pH high too!). You can prevent these infections and keep your vaginal pH balance healthy by not douching and keeping semen out of the vagina.

During the last part of the exam, your health care provider will do a bimanual exam. He or she will place one or two lubricated gloved fingers into your vagina while gently pressing on your abdomen with the other hand. Your health care provider will feel your vaginal canal, uterus, and ovaries to check for any abnormal masses or tenderness that could be from an infection or unusual growth on the ovaries or uterus. Although pelvic exams may seem a little frightening at first, they can answer important questions you have about your body and reproductive health.

••

My first pelvic exam

I was pretty nervous during my first pelvic exam. It was embarrassing to have that part of my body so exposed, but actually the exam didn't hurt at all. The doctor explained each step as she went along. She showed me how to use my breathing to relax my body so I now know exactly what to do during my next exam to feel comfortable and relaxed. I had this vaginal discharge I was really worried about, so it was such a relief when the doctor said it was perfectly normal!

••

If your pelvic exam results are not normal, your health care provider will talk to you about the next steps for treatment. For more information on the pelvic and other important exams, like the breast self-exam for breast cancer, check out: http://www.youngwomenshealth.org/healthinfo.html

The website http://www.komen.org/bse will show you how to do a breast self-examination.

SOCIAL RELATIONSHIPS

Your relationships with other people are an important part of your social life. But, before you can have relationships with other people, you must recognize your own individuality. Individuality is the sum of qualities that characterize and distinguish you from other people. Acknowledging your own individuality is not only *knowing* who you are, but also *accepting* who you are. In terms of any individual characteristic – race, beliefs, goals, body type, social class, etc. – you should never be ashamed of who you are or allow people to make you feel inferior. You must also realize that no one is better than anyone else. Although you may sometimes feel that you can't be the best, or that there are limitations to your dreams, that does not mean that you are inferior. With determination, you can endure and learn from all the obstacles that you may face.

Being comfortable with yourself is the first step in meeting new people. Second, you must be open to meeting new people. In school, for example, getting involved in extracurricular activities is an easy way to make and keep healthy friendships. Extracurricular activities such as sports, theatre, after-school studies, and even community volunteering or religious activities, can turn into "meet and greet" sessions. Some people you come across will just be acquaintances –you know each other but are not close friends. There will also be people who you really connect to, and usually, these people become major parts of your social life.

Learning to Communicate

The ability to communicate with people is essential to everyday life. Communication can be difficult, but lack of communication can make situations even harder. Talking to someone about your thoughts and feelings can help you feel better about your relationships – with your friends, boyfriend, girlfriend, or parents. Believe it or not, good communication can happen even between you and your parents. As long as you remain open to each other's opinions and work toward building a strong friendship and understanding, your parents will be open to your opinions too.

Communication plays an important role in your sexual relationships. It helps you figure out what your partner wants from the relationship – whether it is better conversation, or more sexual intimacy. If you decide to have sex, it is also important to talk to your partner about the risks that come with sexual intimacy and how to prevent pregnancy and sexually transmitted diseases. These can be hard topics to talk about, so it might be a good idea to first get to know your partner before making big decisions, like the decision to have sex. Learning how to communicate better can also bring you and your partner closer, which will make it easier to move to the next phase of your relationship.

Listening, Looking, Leveling, Loving
There is an easy way to teach yourself how to communicate better in any kind of relationship – just remember the Four L's of Communication: Listening, Looking, Leveling, and Loving.

Listening
The first thing to know about communicating is how to listen. Listening is a skill as active as talking, if you do it right. When most people say they're listening, they're actually thinking about what they are going to say as soon as the other person stops talking. When two people do this to each other, there's about as much communicating going on as when you talk back to a radio. So listen to what the other person has to say before you start talking! Don't assume you know what the other person is going to say, and then interrupt before he or she has finished talking. If you do think about interrupting, you're probably not giving that person your full attention.

You can go one step further by deciding not to take personally what the other person is saying to you. Most arguments start because someone else's beliefs or values are different from yours. Some of the things that you say or do can threaten the beliefs of another, and before you know it, an argument begins. In friendship, it is important to learn to respect other people's thoughts and opinions, and in order to do that you must be able to communicate. Another way to avoid taking things too personally is to consider how what you are discussing affects the other person, rather than listening in terms of how it affects you. You can focus on finding a solution through mutual understanding, by thinking about what's best for both of you.

Looking

A second way to improve communication is to make an effort to look at the person who is speaking. This means that you look them in the eyes when you are talking and listening to them. People usually feel you are really listening to what they are saying when you are looking directly at them. Looking doesn't stop with eye contact, however; you can also observe the changes in a person's behavior. For example, when you say something that offends someone, you can usually recognize how the person feels through their facial expressions and body language. Then, the next step should be to try not to say or do things that offend that person or, find out why what you have said upsets them. One of the most important things in any kind of relationship is a consideration for others' feelings, and an ability to reach a common ground with them. Communication, in the end, boils down to learning about another person's way of thinking and their reactions to various topics. In order to communicate well with your partner, you have to learn to pay attention to her or him.

Leveling

Once you begin to listen and observe more effectively in conversation, the next challenge is to learn how to begin discussion by responding appropriately. The best way to do this is to always be honest about what you are feeling. This is called leveling. It is not worth lying to someone just to make them, or you, feel better for the moment. Obviously there are times when it's better to say things in a polite way, or even to keep certain things out of the conversation for both parties' sakes. Even so, your best bet is to be honest about your thoughts and feelings. One way to make sure you do this is to only speak for yourself. When you talk about your feelings instead of the other person's, it's called "owning" your statements. Instead of accusing someone else of general problems ("You don't like being with me."), try talking specifically about your feelings ("I feel left out when you don't call me on the weekends to hang out.") This works well because the person to whom you are talking does not feel attacked, but feels that you are being honest with him or her. The person is more likely to respond in the same way. So instead of saying "you", say "I".

Loving
The last and perhaps most important way to communicate requires love. In everyday conversations, emotions are directed to the listener to help them understand situations. So when you're talking, it helps to consider yourself in the listener's position – what kind of advice or guidance would you want or need to understand the conversation? Just caring about the well-being of another person can help you to communicate better. If you care about them, you won't purposely lead them astray. In most young relationships, the first few months are about getting to know each other better; but as time progresses, a bond of understanding, concern, and consideration should form between you and your partner. Love is an essential part of this bond, which is built through good communication.

Obviously, communicating takes the work of two people. Sometimes, you might be trying to talk to someone who just will not make the effort to meet you halfway. You can tell this person that you feel as if they are being distant and giving you mixed signals. Sometimes this helps to break the ice. Once you've learned to communicate well, you will have a better relationship with yourself, your friends, and your partner.

Talking to Your Parents
Sometimes the hardest people to talk to are your parents. During your teenage years, along with all the changes in your body, your personality will grow, develop, and change. You are changing from a child to an adult, and around this time your lifestyle choices might conflict with what your parents would like. This can result in many disagreements, and you might feel that your parents just do not understand what you're going through. It may that as your experiences and views separate, your relationship gets weaker. But, if you can accept these differences, you and your parents can work together to make the changes easier.

You might think it's difficult to talk to your parents about certain subjects like sex, alcohol, birth control, and drugs. You may be afraid that they will get angry with you – and in many cases, you will be right. Understand that your parents do honestly care and worry about you. When you ask about sex, for example, their prior experiences with the topic can cause them to react in a nervous or concerned way. Sometimes your parents fail to realize that you are growing up, and that if you can't talk to them about these certain subjects, you will be unprepared for similar situations that may occur later in your life. So, in order to keep you aware, these important issues need to be covered in conversations between you and your parents. And if you are not comfortable talking with your parents, find a wise adult you can talk to.

Many people, while growing up, do not realize that their parents can be a wonderful source of knowledge. Having a good relationship with your parents can be a great asset because they offer an opinion of someone who truly cares about you, and they might have different views from your friends. The more perspectives you can take on an issue, the more you will be able to consider it from all angles before making a decision. Statistics even show that children who can talk to their parents comfortably about sexual subjects are more likely to be responsible about birth control when they have sex.* The effort to establish good communication between you and your parents might be difficult, but it's worth it.

It is important to realize that your parents may not always react the way you want. After all, they are people with feelings, and it is important to respect that. Sometimes discussing their concerns for you can help ease some of their fears. Tell your parents how you are feeling emotionally about sex, or promise them that if you are ever in a dangerous situation, you will call them. There is a good solution to most difficult situations, and in the case of parent/child relationships, communication is necessary for these solutions.

---

*Adapted from "A Time to Talk," an educational program developed by Organon, Inc.

Having a good relationship with your parents involves the participation of both people. Sometimes you have to tell your parents that you feel they need to be more understanding of your needs. If you do this in a non-aggressive manner, hopefully they will respect your needs. If situations don't seem to improve and you've done everything you know to do, seek professional advice for yourself and with your parents.

YOUR REPRODUCTIVE LIFE PLAN

Ask Yourself These Questions...
All throughout life, people make plans. They make plans every day, such as what to have for dinner and what to do Saturday night. They make long-term plans for the future, such as whether or not to go to college and what kind of work they want to do. Making plans is an important part of everyone's life.

During the teenage years, when your body, sexual/romantic relationships, and attitudes toward sex are developing, it is important to think about your plan for how sex or having children (if you choose to) will fit into your life. Such a plan might be called a personal, or reproductive, life plan. A reproductive life plan helps you think about important long-term decisions, such as: whether or not you want to get married (and if so, when), whether or not you want to have children (and if so, when and how many), and how these life events might be balanced with your education, work, and personal relationships.

A reproductive life plan also helps you think about when you want to start having sex. Questions on this topic include: under what conditions you want to have sex, with whom you want to have sex, what methods of birth control (if any) fit into your lifestyle and reproductive life plan, how these birth control needs might change between different periods in your life, and how you would deal with an unplanned pregnancy.

The following questions are adapted from a book called **It's Your Choice**. They can help you think about the choices that make up your reproductive life plan. As you complete the survey, remember that there are no "right" or "wrong" answers. There are, however, safe and responsible things you can do to help you follow your plan. For example, if you plan to have sex right now, but you don't want children for another ten years, it is a good idea to choose an effective (perhaps long-term) method of birth control. Or, if you're in a relationship and you don't want to have sex right now, discuss your plans with your boyfriend or girlfriend, and date only those people who respect your choices.

NOTE: This exercise is equally important for MEN and WOMEN. If you think you have found a long-term partner, answer these questions separately and then compare notes. Talk about your differences, and discuss how well the two reproductive life plans could fit together.

Part I: Reproductive Life Planning

Would I like to be married one day?

> If yes, at what age would I like to be married if I could have this happen whenever I wanted?

Would I like to have children one day?

> If yes, how old would I like to be when I have my first child, and how many children would I like to have?

Would I be sad if I were not able to have any children?

Would I like to wait until I'm married to start having sex?

Would I like to wait until I'm married to have children?

How many years of formal education would I like to complete?

At what point during or after my education would I like to be married?

Would I like to work when my children are infants and toddlers?

> When they are in their childhood years? When they no longer live at home?

Of all the things I could do in my life, probably the most important for me to accomplish is this:

Children would affect this goal in the following ways:

What would it mean to me if my marriage ended in divorce?

How does my life plan fit in with my ethical or religious beliefs?

Am I doing what I feel is right for me to do?

How would I feel about having sex with someone other than my partner or spouse?

How would I feel about my partner or spouse having sex with someone else?

Part II: Reproductive Decisions For The Teen Years
In what ways do I feel comfortable expressing myself sexually?

Do I want to have sex before I get married?

Do I want to become pregnant before I get married? If I were to become pregnant in my teen years, what would I do?

Part 2:
Human Sexuality

HUMAN SEXUALITY

People experience sexuality through relationships with others and through their own fantasies. A person's ideas and feelings about sexuality are also influenced by the media and the press, which use sex and sexual symbols to get people to buy products (beer, cars, perfumes), adopt certain opinions (about political candidates and organizations), and behave in certain ways (smoke cigarettes, go to a particular restaurant, play a sport). But in the real world, human sexuality is very different from what we see in the media; sexuality has nothing to do with the perfume you wear or the sport you play. This section of the book will describe the different aspects of sex in a realistic and straightforward way.

As you begin to learn and understand the sexual experiences within and around yourself, you may form beliefs about what is "socially acceptable" sexual behavior. You will also learn about the ways your body physically responds to sexual emotions. Exploring sexuality can be fun and exciting because there are many ways to find enjoyment and satisfaction in your sex life; all it takes is some interest, information, and experimentation.

Enjoying your sexuality depends, to a large extent, on communication and education. It is crucial that you talk about sexuality with your partner, friends, and family. It is equally important to take responsibility and learn about topics involving your own sexuality.

Let's Talk About Sex...

High school is a learning experience for everyone. At this point in your life, the word "sex" is an important issue that is brought up in everyday life and in school. The word "sex" can mean lots of different things. A lot of people think that "sex" refers to penis-in-vagina or penis-in-anus intercourse, but many others believe that "sex" is not limited to intercourse. People also make different decisions about different types of sex. For example, some decide to abstain from sexual intercourse and find pleasure in other ways. It is okay to choose abstinence or masturbation instead of sex.

In this section, "sex" is defined to mean everything from casual touching to all kinds of intercourse (vaginal, anal, and oral). The purpose of this section is to help you understand the different ways people express their sexuality.

Just as people have individual personalities, people have individual sexual needs. What makes some people very excited may not be a turn on for others. It is important to be respectful of your partner's wants and wishes as well as your own. There is nothing dirty or wrong with making yourself feel good, as long as you are comfortable with what you are doing, you do it privately, and without hurting others. Your actions must be thought through in terms of your personal value system. Everyone makes different decisions about sex. For example, some decide to abstain from sexual intercourse and find pleasure in other ways. It is always okay to choose abstinence instead of sex.

Sexual Arousal & Response

Affectionate Touching
People enjoy physical contact. After all, people are social beings. Friends touch each other affectionately through hugging, back rubs, or congratulatory slaps on the back. Touching can also be a nice form of communication between couples. Holding hands, kissing (with or without tongues), and gentle caresses are all ways that people can express their feelings for each other. Our society generally finds this sort of touching acceptable in public. Even when you are alone together, touching can also be a great way to show someone you care.

Kissing
You probably kiss people all the time, including your parents, friends, family, and partner. For many people, the first time they hear about French kissing (tongue to tongue, or tongue in mouth) they are a little disgusted. Some people will continue to feel uncomfortable kissing – and that's fine, because there are many other ways to show affection for someone. For those people who do think they might enjoy kissing, many get nervous or scared about their first experience French kissing or kissing a certain person. But even if at first your noses collide, mouths miss or suddenly you have to sneeze, kissing is a form of expression that

couples can explore and learn together. It can get better, more relaxed, and even fun! There are lots of different ways to kiss someone – be creative!

"Fooling Around"

"Fooling around", "messing around" and "making out" are terms often used for things people do that are sexual and fun, but do not usually include intercourse of any kind. "Fooling around" may include touching, kissing and caressing, rubbing your partner's genitals or any other parts of the body that feels good. Many people, both males and females, can have orgasms from stimulating or rubbing the genitals.

"Fooling around" can be very satisfying and enjoyable. There are many parts of the human body called erogenous zones, which are sensitive to touching or other types of stimulation like changes in temperature. Each person has his or her own sensitive areas that can be aroused by touch. Arousal spots vary in location on every person, and may include the back of the ears, the inner knees, the neck, and between the toes. It is important to be aware of your partner's sensitive areas, and also of your own. With time you will learn to tell each other what you like, what feels good, and what doesn't.

Intercourse

Intercourse is a very physical and intimate kind of sex between two people. There are three different kinds of intercourse: vaginal (penis-in-vagina), anal (penis-in-anus), and oral (mouth-to-penis, mouth-to-vagina, mouth-to-anus). Intercourse, like any other part of sex, can be an intense emotional and physical experience.

Many people find that the decision to have intercourse is a difficult one to make, especially because it might result in pregnancy (vaginal intercourse) and infection (all kinds of intercourse). For more information on making this decision, see Saying "Yes" or "No" to Sexual Intimacy (page 71). Whether or not you want to have intercourse right now, here are some important things to know about it.

Vaginal (Penis-in-Vagina) Intercourse

Intercourse

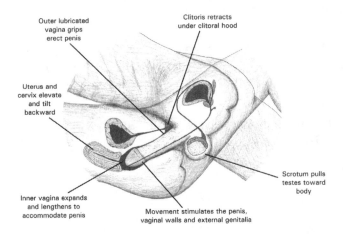

Outer lubricated vagina grips erect penis

Clitoris retracts under clitoral hood

Uterus and cervix elevate and tilt backward

Scrotum pulls testes toward body

Inner vagina expands and lengthens to accommodate penis

Movement stimulates the penis, vaginal walls and external genitalia

In the first kind of intercourse – vaginal or penis-in-vagina – the man's penis is put into the woman's vagina. The vagina is not a huge hollow cavity where the penis can get lost or go in the wrong way. The opening to the vagina can actually be a little tight or dry (especially if it is a woman's first time or if she is not sexually excited and moist), and it might take a while for the penis to get inside. If it is a woman's first time having vaginal intercourse, she should not be surprised if she has some bleeding after the penis enters the vagina. This is normal and happens because the hymen, a circle of tissue that partly covers the opening of the vagina, stretches and sometimes tears. Many women don't have bleeding the first time a penis enters the vagina and that is normal too. Sometimes the hymen gets stretched on its own before vaginal intercourse. Instead of rushing to push the penis in, try stimulating each other some more until the vagina is well lubricated. If the rubbing of the penis on the vagina is hurting the woman, it may be because she is not wet enough. A lubricant can be put on the penis, in and around the vagina, or on a condom to make everything more slippery and to help the penis to slide in comfortably. Warning: Never use Vaseline® or oils with either a latex condom or a diaphragm – it rots the rubber and may cause a latex condom to break. Many drug stores sell lubricants that can be used for sex, and many condoms are sold lubricated. Some favorite lubricants are Astroglide®, Slippery Stuff®, and K-Y® Jelly, which you can buy at any drug store without a prescription. **Following is a list of safe and unsafe lubricants to use with latex condoms and dental dams**.

Safe, water-based lubricants keep condoms and dental dams from breaking by reducing friction. **Safe** lubricants are:
- Water
- Saliva
- Spermicide/nonoxynol 9* such as Gynol II®
- Glycerin
- Egg whites
- Aloe-9
- Aqua lube®
- Silicone lubricant
- H-R® lubricant
- PrePair®
- Ramses® Personal lubricant
- Touch®
- Wet®
- Astroglide®
- K-Y® Jelly
- Probe®
- EROS (silicone based)

*Do not use spermicide or spermicidally lubricated condoms for anal intercourse

Unsafe, oil-based lubricants can damage latex condoms and cause them to break or leak. **Unsafe** lubricants that you should NOT use with latex condoms or dams are:
- Baby oil
- Cold creams
- Body Butters/Shea Butter
- Bag Balm®
- Cornhuskers lubricant®
- Edible oils (olive oil, peanut oil, corn oil, sunflower oil, coconut oil, butter, etc.)
- Hand/body lotion
- Massage oil
- Petroleum jelly/Vaseline®

- Rubbing alcohol
- Suntan oil/lotion
- Vegetable/mineral oil
- Vaginal infection creams/suppositories (e.g. Monistat® or Terazol®)
- Chocolate syrup
- Crisco
- Whipped cream/ice cream

Vaginal (penis-in-vagina) intercourse usually continues with the couple positioning themselves so that the penis can move in and out of the vagina, until the man reaches an orgasm ("comes"). A man reaches orgasm when the semen that has built up spurts out, or is ejaculated. Although many women can have an orgasm from the rubbing of the penis in the vagina, many others need direct stimulation of their clitoris in order to have an orgasm. Since the clitoris is outside of the vagina and above the opening where the penis enters, the man may need to use his hand to help her have an orgasm (or she can rub her own clitoris while his penis is inside her).

It is not necessary for both people to reach orgasm at the same time – in fact, it's a little unrealistic. Intercourse should be pleasurable for both people, and there is no rule that says each person must have an orgasm every time for this to happen. Sometimes it can be pleasurable just to know that you are giving another person pleasure.

There is no right or wrong position for having vaginal intercourse. It can be done standing up, with the woman on top, with the man on top, side by side, or with the man putting his penis into the woman's vagina from behind. Contrary to popular belief, a couple can have vaginal intercourse when the woman is having her period. Some women find that having vaginal intercourse and/or an orgasm during their period reduces their menstrual cramps. However, if a woman or man feels uncomfortable with having vaginal intercourse when the woman is bleeding, for either religious or personal beliefs, then these feelings should be respected.

If you or your partner do not want to get pregnant, it is important to use contraception during vaginal intercourse. It is also essential to use a condom if you both want to avoid getting a sexually transmitted disease (see page 82 on Choosing a Contraceptive Method and page 143 on AIDS and Other Sexually Transmitted Diseases).

Other Kinds of Intercourse
Anal sex is when a man puts his penis inside another person's anus (butt). Anal sex can be between two men or between a man and a woman. In anal sex, it is necessary to use a lubricant because the anus is a small cavity and it does not create its own lubricant like the vagina does. There are many risks with anal sex because the skin is fragile. Even when using lots of lubrication, the delicate skin of the anus can tear and bleed during anal sex. Since most sexually transmitted diseases spread through fluid exchange, this type of sexual intercourse, especially without using a condom, can be risky. Whether performed between a man and a woman or two men, anal sex has the same risks.

Oral sex is when one person puts his or her mouth or tongue onto or into his or her partner's genitals. When oral sex is performed on a woman (i.e. the mouth and tongue are used to stimulate the clitoris and vagina), it is called cunnilingus or "eating out" or "going down". When oral sex is performed on a man (the mouth and tongue stimulate the penis), it is called fellatio – or a "blow job" or "giving head". Men and women can perform both cunnilingus and fellatio on their partners, depending on the partner's sex.

Another type of oral sex is when one person puts his or her mouth or tongue onto or into the anus of another person. This is sometimes called oral-anal intercourse or "rimming."

Different types of intercourse may sound a little disgusting to many people, and there are many churches and other groups that are against these sorts of activities before marriage. On the other hand, many people enjoy oral sex as part of foreplay, or anal sex as an alternative to vaginal intercourse. Whether or not you personally like or approve of these forms of sexual intimacy, it is important for you to know that others may find them pleasurable (see Sexual Diversity, page 68).

Although you cannot get pregnant from oral sex, and it is unlikely that you will get pregnant from anal sex, it is still very possible to get sexually transmitted diseases from all of these activities. If you are not comfortable with the idea of oral or anal sex, you should not allow anyone to pressure you into doing or experiencing something you don't like. The diagram below shows which sexually intimate activities are more or less risky when it comes to passing sexually transmitted diseases.

STDs (Sexually Transmitted Diseases)
Safest to Riskiest Behaviors Range

SAFEST   RISKIEST

| Hugging, Touching over clothes, Touching | Kissing closed mouth | Touching each other under clothes (not genitals) | Kissing open mouth (French kissing) | Touching each others' genitals under clothes | Rubbing your genitals against another | Oral sex (mouth on penis or vagina) | Intercourse or penis in vagina | Mouth on anus (oral anal sex) | Anal sex (penis in anus) |

Masturbation

Masturbation is when you or your partner use hands or other objects to stimulate your own clitoris, penis, breast or nipples, or anus for pleasure. Often when people masturbate, they do it until they have an orgasm. Masturbation can leave a person feeling good, relieved, or relaxed.

However, some people don't like masturbation because they feel guilty or embarrassed about giving sexual pleasure to themselves. They might have grown up learning that touching their genitals is "wrong," or heard various myths associated with masturbation that say it causes warts, blindness, or three-headed children. These stories are all untrue! Most people consider masturbation a completely natural, normal, and harmless way to enjoy yourself. Masturbation is a good way to learn about sexual stimulation and how your body functions sexually.

Some benefits of masturbation are that:
- It can end with an orgasm.
- It can be done alone, or with another person.
- It's a satisfying and simple means of relieving tension or stress.
- It may decrease menstrual pain (following an orgasm).
- It requires no birth control.
- It has no risk of sexually transmitted diseases (STDs).

Some people feel that masturbation is a good place to start exploring your sexuality, because it can help you to figure out your own sexual likes and dislikes, and it does not come with risks of infection or pregnancy. However, everyone is different – nobody should be expected or compelled to masturbate, and not all people enjoy stimulating themselves. People can explore various types of sexual intimacy to have fun and find what's most effective for them, and that's perfectly natural. Whether or not you masturbate is a personal choice.

Sexual Arousal and Response

Remember, sex can be whatever you and your partner make it. According to Master's and Johnson, sexual arousal and response is divided into four physical stages: excitement, plateau, orgasm and resolution. According to Helen Singer Kaplan there is an additional stage in the beginning of the sexual response cycle called "desire." Each stage is described below:

Desire
Desire or libido is a stage in which a man or a woman begins to want or "desire" sexual intimacy or pleasure. This stage may last from a moment to many years.

Excitement
The excitement stage is when a couple first become sexually stimulated. Most people have some form of sexual foreplay – kissing, teasing, caressing, and massaging – to get "turned on" before, or instead of, intercourse. Any part of the body can be sensitive to sexual stimulation, but areas such as the penis, clitoris, thighs, buttocks, breasts, nipples, neck and ears are highly sensitive. A back rub can be extremely exciting. People are such "sexual beings" that almost anything can turn them on!

Since sexual pleasure varies from person to person, it is crucial to communicate with your partner about sexual comforts and preferences. When you and your partner let each other know your likes and dislikes, you will probably be more satisfied with your relationship. After all, when you make the choice to have sex, you want it to be enjoyable for both you and your partner.

Male Excitement Phase

Female Excitement Phase

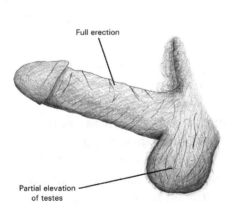

Full erection

Partial elevation of testes

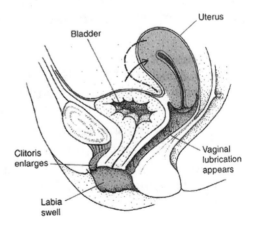

Uterus

Bladder

Clitoris enlarges

Vaginal lubrication appears

Labia swell

The excitement stage can continue for as long as the couple wants. You can tell when a person is in the excitement stage because a man's penis will get an erection (get hard) and a women's vagina will lubricate (get wet). Along with these physical changes, both partners will have increased heart and breathing rates.

Male Plateau Phase   Female Plateau Phase

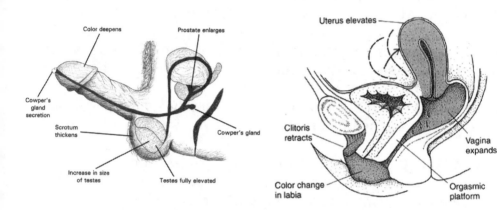

Plateau
The plateau stage is the very pleasurable period of time when orgasm seems inevitable. The changes in the body that begin in the excitement stage increase during the plateau stage and can last from minutes to sometimes hours.

Orgasm
An orgasm is the third stage, and many people consider it the "high point" of sexual activity and excitement. Both men and women, at the time of orgasm, have a series of pleasurable muscle contractions, especially in the penis and vagina. A man ejaculates (comes) when he has reached an orgasm, and semen will spurt out through the penis usually several times before the orgasm is completed. The total volume of an ejaculate is about a teaspoonful. A woman has an orgasm when her sexual body

parts have been stimulated enough, usually by friction between the bodies and sexual organs. Orgasms vary – they may be eruptions of hollering ecstasy, or they may be a simple gush of relief. Movies and novels depict people having orgasms with enough contortions to break the bed frame. An orgasm may be like that, or it may be just a sweet sigh in the night.

Male Orgasm Phase

Female Orgasm Phase

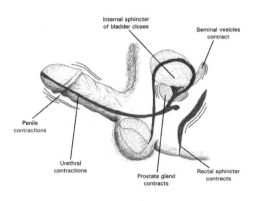

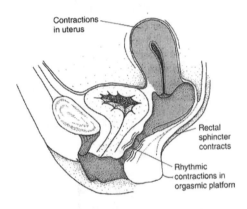

Both men and women sometimes worry that they will not be able to sexually please their partner. Many men worry about penis size. However, when the man is excited and his penis swells with blood (erection), it increases in size and hardness. Women might also worry about the stretchiness or wetness of their vaginal walls, and lubricants can help a lot. At the start of intercourse a woman's vagina is somewhat tight, and it expands or stretches to be large enough to fit around the penis. Whatever size the man's penis is, it will be touching the most sensitive part of the woman's vagina – the first outer third, which is not very long; the inner two-thirds of the vaginal walls have little feeling in most women. So regardless of the size of the man's penis or the wetness of the woman's vagina, sex can be an exciting experience for both partners. And, simply the sensuality and closeness of having intercourse can be enough to cause orgasm!

Resolution or Decline
In the fourth stage, the resolution or decline period, all the previous physical changes (increased heartbeat, skin flushing, penis erection, swelling of the clitoris and the lips of the vagina, return to normal. Most people feel a sense of relief and/or calmness.

Male Resolution Phase   Female Resolution Phase

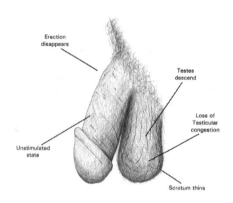

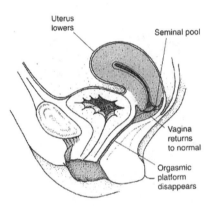

Refractory Period
Men have a refractory period after sexual intercourse, when erection is not possible. This may last for a few minutes to a few days depending on age, physical condition, and emotional state. Women do not have a refractory period and can have several orgasms in succession.

Of course, there is no rule saying that you must have an orgasm to have a good time. Many couples enjoy just kissing, touching, or holding each other without having an orgasm. Whatever you decide to do, make sure that there is clear communication and nobody gets hurt. The most important thing to consider is how comfortable you and your partner are about having sex.

SEXUAL DIVERSITY

The last section discussed what people do with each other sexually. Just as there is a lot of diversity in sexual behaviors, there is also a lot of diversity in gender identity, sexual attraction and relationships. Your gender identity is how you feel on the inside - male or female or a mixture of both. This sense of your inside gender usually develops when you are a child. Not everyone who looks like a male on the outside feels like a male on the inside and the same can be true for females. When a person's inside gender feelings do not match their outside sexual organs or internal chromosomes, it is called transgender. Transgender is also used as a broad term to describe anyone who crosses or transcends traditional gender boundaries. Someone who alters in part or total their external body parts to match their inside gender identity is called transsexual.

Your sexual orientation is who you are sexually or physically attracted to. Sexual orientations are often given names that describe the sex of the person to whom you are attracted since you can be physically or sexually attracted to people of the same sex, the opposite sex or both.

Heterosexual attraction is between two people of opposite sexes: male and female. Homosexual attraction is between two people of the same sex: male and male, or female and female.

Bisexual attraction is when a person is sexually attracted to both men and women. The teen years are a common time to wonder about your sexual feelings, what they mean, and how they help you define who you are as a sexual person.

It is important to keep in mind that just because a person is attracted to someone of a particular sex (same, opposite, or both), that does not mean that they have sexual activities with people of that sex. A person may choose not to identify themselves as gay (homosexual), straight (heterosexual), or bi (bisexual). In fact, it is completely normal to feel attracted to people of the same sex at certain times in your life, yet that does not automatically make you gay. The same is true if you are attracted to people of the opposite sex or both sexes; it does not mean that you are definitely heterosexual or bisexual for the rest of your life. People's sexual attractions develop over the years and can change a lot over a lifetime.

Some people might believe that anything other than heterosexuality is unnatural, but other people believe that homosexuality and bisexuality are natural and healthy. Nobody knows to what extent homosexuality is a choice or biologically determined, but it is certainly all a part of being an individual. Even if you have a different sexual orientation than someone else, you do not have the right to discriminate against them because of their individual sexual orientation, choice or practices.

Exploring Sexuality
Even though there is no way to tell by looking at a person what their sexual orientation or identity is, society tries to categorize people based on who they have sex with. In reality, though, this is impossible, because we all have unique and very complex sexualities. The range of human diversity is limitless, and many people have explored attractions to same- and opposite-sex people in their lifetimes. This section is included to help you understand your feelings during those times when you may question your sexual orientation and identity.

Your sexual orientation is a major part of your sexual identity, so only you can decide what is right and comfortable for you. You may not fit completely into just one of society's sexuality categories (heterosexual, homosexual, bisexual), and you shouldn't feel like you have to. What is important is that you develop a sexual orientation that you feel comfortable with. Each person will define his or her sexual identity and attractions differently, by a combination of psychological, emotional, and social factors. Some books and places to call for support are listed in the resource section at the end of the book.
The Hetrick-Martin Institute
212-674-2400

Indianapolis Youth Group
800-347-TEEN

Lavender Youth Recreation and Information Center
415-863-3636 (San Francisco area 800-246-PRIDE)

Parents and Friends of Lesbians and Gays (PFLAG)
202-638-4200

Coming Out

At some point in life, everyone has some questions about their sexual orientation and wonders how to define themselves. *Your sexual orientation can be defined in any way you choose.* By no means is it based solely on who your sexual partners are. Many people define their sexual orientation as who they feel sexually or physically attracted to. These feelings can develop long before a first sexual act or experience takes place.

Many people are curious about their feelings for members of the same sex. Some people will conclude that they want to be sexual only with men, some only with women, and some will want emotional and sexual relationships with both sexes. This conclusion may lead to a sexual orientation that is difficult to accept, and the process of coming out to oneself, or accepting one's sexual identity, can take time. Eventually, a person may also feel the need to explain these thoughts and feelings to friends and family. For people who call themselves heterosexual, this is usually not very difficult, since our culture accepts this as a way of life. For people who are interested in members of their own sex, this can be a very troubling time.

The process of acknowledging oneself as gay, lesbian, or bisexual is often called "coming out." Although it can be self-affirming and provide some sense of relief, coming out can also make a person feel scared and vulnerable. Coming out can be a life-long experience. Once a person finds and accepts a sexual orientation and identity, he or she may want to come out to others, such as parents, siblings, or friends. There are many opportunities for coming out. Who to come out to is an individual decision.

It is important to be aware that coming out can be a very emotional process. Having a support network of friends and/or family members can be very helpful to a person trying to come out. People who are part of somebody's support system should realize that everyone copes with coming out differently. Factors such as race, gender, religious background, and how much money your family has can influence the coming out experience, and make it easier or harder. The fears of coming out may include loss of financial support, loss of emotional support, being disowned or thrown out by one's family, losing friendships, and being alienated or isolated. Reactions to "coming out" can be both positive and negative, so having a good support system is very helpful.

SAYING "YES" OR "NO" TO SEXUAL INTIMACY

The purpose of this section is *not* to encourage you to say "yes" or "no" to sex; it is to help you think about what you want and why. Since everybody can think of reasons – some good and others not so good – for why people have sex, it might help to consider your own reasons for saying "yes" or "no" to sex. Sex can bring you pleasure, fun, passion, and closeness, and it may be a way to show someone that you love them or care about them. Sex can cause emotional pain and suffering. Painful feelings about sex are some of the hardest emotions that people – young or old – have to cope with. Having sex before you are ready or with the wrong person may cause long-term grief and regret.

There are many factors that go into the decision to have a sexual relationship. For instance, you should consider your emotional stability and the stability of your relationship. How do you feel about your potential partner? Do you love him or her? How does he or she feel about you? Are you using sex to win affection, to prove love, or to keep the relationship going? Remember that sex is not just a physical act! It often brings on many different emotions, some of which you may not be ready for, especially if you are emotionally insecure about your relationship.

It is very important to consider how sex will affect the other parts of your life, such as career, school, and sports. Getting involved sexually with another person can shift your focus away from important goals, limit your freedom, or simply interfere with your life. It's a good idea to consider the consequences of your decision for you as an individual, as someone with a future that may not include your partner. Will sex limit your personal goals and accomplishments?

It's Your Choice

The choices you make about sex or any form of sexual intimacy are yours – not your parents', your friend's, your religion's, your boyfriend's or girlfriend's, but YOURS. No one can tell you what is right or wrong for you because you are the only one who knows your needs, values, and desires. Talking to someone else about your thoughts and feelings may help you sort things out, but the final decision is entirely yours.

Finding the right answers means acknowledging your individuality. This may be hard, considering that things are changing inside and around you, and that other people may want you to make different decisions.

Conflicting Voices

Ruth Bell, author of *Changing Bodies, Changing Lives*, says that the opinions of people who influence your sexual behavior are like voices inside your head. Imagine that inside your head, there is a constant conversation between many "voices," each with an opinion about what you should do. As you are deciding whether or not to be sexually intimate, these voices may pressure and confuse you with their different messages. The following voices represent some of the opinions that you might hear.

Voice One: Your Parents

Even if your parents haven't talked to you specifically about sex, you probably have a good idea of how they feel. If your parents are very protective, they may feel you will be hurt by getting infections, becoming or getting someone pregnant, or getting hurt when an emotional relationship ends. They may expect you to be a virgin for the rest of your life and their message may not be very realistic. If they fear your sexuality or don't want you to be sexual at all, you may be tempted to tune out their voices.

Sometimes your parents' voices may be strong enough to make you feel guilty. But if your parents trust your judgment and only want you to take care of yourself, their advice can be very helpful. Whatever their message, regardless of whether or not you agree with it, listen closely! Your parents' opinions may not always be right, but their feeling about you are strong and powerful, and this is a voice you should be aware of.

Voice Two: Your Friends

Your friends' voices are probably very important to you right now. They may differ depending on whether you're a guy or a girl and on what kind of people you hang out with. You might feel pressured when you hear things like, "Did you hit that yet?" or "Can't you get it up?" These voices suggest that you should be having sex whether you want to or not. But remember to consider how these comments make your partner feel. What does your partner mean to you? Is having sex going to help you build the type of relationship you want? Are you performing for your friends, or do you want to make yourself happy? You may also hear warning voices that say, "Watch out, or it will ruin your reputation!" or "Do you want to be called a slut?" Once again, think about yourself and your own values, not what other people think about you. Whatever direction the pressure is coming from, remember it's your life and your choice.

Voice Three: Religious Attitudes and Beliefs

For many people, religious attitudes are very important. Many religions believe that sex outside of marriage is sinful. Unfortunately, sometimes when a religious group says "No," the opinion is so strong that it doesn't permit you to think through your own feelings and decide for yourself the rightness or wrongness of the issue. As a result, this may cause you to feel tremendous guilt, or to react by doing just the opposite. Reflect on your own value system, and think about what is important to you. What sort of decision will make you feel good, happy, and proud? What kinds of decisions might make you feel unhappy, guilty, or regretful?

Voice Four: The Media

TV, magazines, and movies usually give us the idea that the only way to be a completely successful person is to be beautiful and sexy. For a woman to be "hot" or a man to be a "player", they seem to say that you have to know all the moves, lines, and facts about sex.

But the media represents a fantasy world! They are trying to sell you sex to make money. The love scenes you see on the screen are not realistic images for most people. If you try to live up to the expectations of the media, you are likely to be disappointed in yourself. Also, the common mixing of violence and sex in television and movies provides negative and unhealthy "sex education" to our society. Just because rape and forced violence are portrayed as erotic on the television or movie screen, this *in no way* means that these behaviors are acceptable for anyone!!

Voice Five: Your Own Needs
Your own feelings and needs are the most important inner voice you will hear. If it seems that you are listening only to the other voices, try listening harder to yourself. Even though your needs may be confusing at the moment, they will become clearer with time.

Although it may seem that sex is the answer to some of your needs, think about those needs before you get involved. Remember, sex is not the right way to resolve an argument, make someone else jealous, or find love. If affection, reassurance, or acceptance is what you really need, sex is not the answer.

Voice Six: Your Own Standards
Your standards may change as you grow, but deciding what they are now can be very useful. Standards give you guidelines even before you start a relationship. As you grow and have relationships, the voice of your own standards will get wiser and stronger, and you'll come to trust that voice more. You will learn what your limits are, what you can handle, and what seems right for you.

Balancing the Voices
Hearing more than one of these voices at a time challenges how well you will know yourself, and how strongly you will stand up for yourself. It will be hard to satisfy all the voices, but as you get older and gain more experience, you'll find it easier to make decisions. Hopefully, you will be able to weigh your voice against all others and come up with what's right for you. If you are in doubt, think about your decision carefully, or talk it over with someone you trust. Don't do anything you are not sure you want to do and don't feel is right for you.

Things I Wouldn't Even Consider...

Sometimes it is hard to make clear decisions about what's best for you at the time the decision needs to be made. Emotions, peer pressure, and alcohol or drugs can cloud your judgment. That's why it is a good idea to make certain decisions ahead of time, when you are not being influenced by all of these factors. A good way to do this is to make a list of things that you would not consider doing. Here's a list that other people your age came up with when asked what they would never consider doing in a sexual situation:

They said they wouldn't even consider...

...having sex when they didn't want to.

...having unprotected sex.

...not using birth control when they were not ready to get pregnant.

...lying to a sexual partner.

...believing that just because they've been with someone for a long time that they have to have sex.

...believing that just because they had sex with someone before that they need to keep having sex with them.

...believing that just because they had sex in the past that they need to have sex in all their future relationships.

...having sex with someone for fear of losing them if they don't.

...having sex to get back at another person who upset them.

...not stopping when a partner says "no" or "stop."

...thinking "it won't happen to me."

...believing that they can't get pregnant the first time.

...having sex when they or their partner was drunk.

...raping someone, or forcing themselves on someone.

We have left some space below so that you can write your own "Things I wouldn't Even Consider..." list. Remember, this list is only for you – you can write down whatever you feel is right for you.

_____

_____

_____

_____

_____

_____

_____

_____

Let's Be Honest

Try to be honest with yourself. Lots of people have sex for personal reasons that have nothing to do with sex. Here are some of the reasons that people have sex:

- They're curious.
- They want to hold onto a relationship that is breaking up.
- They are lonely and unhappy and they think sex can make them feel close to someone.
- They want to lose their virginity.
- They want to prove to their parents and society that they're independent or grown-up.
- They had sex once and they think there is no point in holding back now.
- They think everyone else is doing it.
- They want to be popular.

These are not healthy or wise reasons to have sex. There are better ways to prove your commitment to a relationship, or to prove yourself to your friends, than by having sex. Of course, it is totally natural to be curious about sex and to have sexual desires; after all, during the adolescent years, hormones are creating strong feelings in your body. But hormones aren't everything! Your hormones can't think for you, so you need to use your brains to think through your emotions and feelings and figure out what is right for you. If you don't, you may get hurt.

TEN RULES OF SEXUAL ETIQUETTE*

Young adults today face a sexual environment that has changed drastically over the past 35 or 40 years. The birth control pill, the legalization of abortion, and the widespread threat of HIV, AIDS, and other sexually transmitted diseases are a few of the most dramatic changes. As part of this new environment, sexuality is more openly discussed. At the same time, over 80% of never-married U.S. teenagers have had intercourse by the age of 20. The new openness about sex and the greater threat of physical danger from sex suggests a need for increased education and responsibility, better communication, and more respect for individuals.

What is Sexual Etiquette?

Each society has its own rules of etiquette. Because sexual relationships tend to be private, there is an assumption that we do not need rules about thoughtfulness and respect for others when dealing with sexual issues. *This could not be further from the truth.*

Practical guidelines can help people think about sex and its consequences, protect themselves and their partners, and even enjoy their relationship more. Developing a personal code of sexual behavior can help you avoid getting hurt and hurting others in a relationship.

Ten Suggested Rules of Sexual Etiquette

The 10 "Rules of Sexual Etiquette" are derived from common sense, a respect for your personal/sexual needs and choices, and a concern for the feelings of others. These rules are suggestions – not a list of strict do's and don't's.

1. Be sure both of you want to be sexual.

Coercion (forcing or tricking someone into doing something they are not comfortable with) can take many forms. Whether you are on a first date or married and have agreed to have sex, coercing a person to do something is wrong.

Many times, men and women do not see their actions as coercive, yet coercion can come about in many ways. Using emotions or words to pressure someone to have sex, or using physical strength to overpower another person can result in sexual assault.

2. If he or she does <u>not</u> say "Yes" to sex, it means "No."

At any time in a sexual relationship, either person has the right to say "No." "No" does not mean "Keep going, I was just kidding." Nor does "No" mean "Try harder, you may convince me." If a woman or man says "No," the answer should be respected without question; "No" means "No," not "Maybe." Also, never assume a "Yes" response until the person has said it clearly and without pressure.

••

Questions about date rape

I do not understand what date rape is. One time, I was with this girl who said "No." I did not hold her down or force her, but after nibbling her ear she consented to having sex. Later I felt like I had raped her. It made me uncomfortable and our relationship ended. Did I rape her or did she really change her mind?

••

A person can say "No" without actually saying the word "No." Even if someone does not say "No," it does not mean they have said "Yes." Always make sure that you and your partner are both consensual about what you are doing together; that way, nobody will get hurt. If you are unsure at all about how either of you feels, like in the case above, take the time to talk about it.

If someone says "No" and is pressured to give reasons, it is unfair and harmful. This type of force will damage the trust that makes intimate relationships positive and fun.

3. In sexual situations, always be thinking ahead.

If you want to stay safe in sexual situations, you will want to think ahead. You can take steps to prevent unwanted things from happening. If there is a small chance that unwanted events will happen, you may want to think about what your choices might be *before* those things really do happen.

Some things are clearly dangerous, walking down a dark alley alone or going into a bedroom with someone you don't know. Other situations may seem harmless, but really they are not. It can be helpful to be aware and think about the safety of your feelings, body, and health.

4. Be aware of your (and his/her) alcohol and drug intake.
When a person is using alcohol and/or drugs, his/her judgment may be impaired. It becomes harder to think clearly and harder to say "No." Resisting force becomes more difficult, and using force becomes more likely. Also, a person under the influence of drugs is more likely to be careless about using condoms and other contraceptives for preventing the spread of infection and avoiding pregnancy.

••

Too much alcohol led to too much pain

We both had too much to drink, and at the end of the evening we wanted to go home together. At my house, we began to fool around. When the point of penetration came, he started hurting me by gripping my wrists and slamming his hips into my inner thighs. I asked him to stop and he only seemed more excited. This experience devastated me and it took me years to overcome it. Now that I know how people can lose control when they're under the influence, I make a point of not being in vulnerable situations with drunk people. That extra little bit of caution has helped me to avoid similar experiences.

••

5. Be prepared.
If there is any chance that you will decide to have sex, be prepared. Have a condom or some other form of birth control with you. If you are not prepared, say "No" or take a rain check. Being prepared does not mean that you are actively looking for

sex or are "a slut." Instead, being prepared simply means you are being safe, realistic, and smart.

•••

Two myths disproved

When I was fourteen, I had sex for the first time. Because it was totally spontaneous we had no protection, and I ended up pregnant. That experience disproved two myths – I learned that you can get pregnant the first time, and that you can get pregnant even if he pulls out.

•••

6. Talk openly.
If you and your partner cannot talk openly about birth control and past sexual activity, you should not be having sex. It is important to know your partner's sexual history and his or her thoughts about birth control, as well as what you both would want if one of you got pregnant accidentally. Your futures really depend on that. Good communication can lead to great relationships, as this case shows.

•••

We talked about abstinence after having sex once

My boyfriend and I had sex for the first time a month ago. We are concerned with pregnancy and diseases. We know our love is strong, and we don't need sex to be happy. That's why we have decided to abstain for now. We have had long talks about our abstinence, and this shared decision made our relationship stronger.

•••

7. Share responsibility in a sexual relationship.
Responsibility should be shared in a sexual relationship. As the saying goes, "It takes two to tango." This means that neither

partner should carry the responsibility alone. In most situations, two people working together can find the best solution to a problem. That might mean that he wears a condom and she uses another type of contraceptive method. In all relationships, both people should share the responsibility and consequences of having a sexual relationship.

8. Respect sexual privacy.
Even though some people like to share their feelings about a relationship with close friends, those "outsiders" do not need explicit details about your and your partner's sexual activity to be able to listen and give advice. Sexual relationships require a high level of trust, and revealing one's sexual activities to another person can seriously harm that trust.

••

My girlfriend's privacy came first

When I first started going out with my girlfriend, all of my buddies on the baseball team kept asking me how far I had gone with her. No matter how much they asked me, though, I didn't feel it was fair to my girlfriend to tell them. Pretty soon they just began to say that I must not have gotten anywhere since I wouldn't talk. Even though those comments seemed endless and could get annoying, I still kept my mouth shut. I wasn't going to sacrifice our trust and privacy just to prove those guys wrong.

••

9. Do not sexually harass other people.
Sexual harassment is not a joke. It is offensive, insensitive, and a violation of personal privacy for both men and women. Pinches and pats, sexual jokes, hints of sexual favors, and sexual comments are all examples of sexual harassment. Essentially, sexual harassment is any unwanted or offensive sexual word or act. Sexual harassment usually occurs when the harasser, who knows that his/her "victim" will not be likely to complain because she/he fears losing something like a job or a friend,

takes advantage of this weakness; it is an abuse of power. Sexual harassment on the job is illegal.

•••

Harassment on the job

When I first started working at this job at a fast food place, I really liked my boss. He was very nice to me and was constantly giving me compliments. Then, it became sort of sexual. He was always touching me and staring at me. I couldn't stand it, but at first I was afraid to say anything to him. I couldn't afford to lose my job. Finally I told him that if he didn't quit it I would report him, and he stopped.

•••

10. Be considerate of others.
Public expressions of sexual intimacy may embarrass or offend other people. You should be aware of, and sensitive to, the feelings of others – keep your public displays of affection to a minimum.

CHOOSING A CONTRACEPTIVE
If you are going to be having intercourse, it is definitely a good time to think about contraception (methods to prevent pregnancy). *Even if you are only thinking about having intercourse, it is a good idea to be prepared.* Talking to your parents, counselors, health care provider, and your partner, as well as reading the next pages, are good ways to start thinking about contraceptives. That way, when the time comes, you will be ready. Difficult as it may be to imagine now, your future can depend on having contraceptives handy and using them correctly. The chances are nearly 9 out of 10 that you will get pregnant in a year, if you have intercourse regularly and don't use anything to prevent pregnancy. Your goals and dreams for the future may depend upon whether or not you and your partner protect yourselves against unplanned pregnancy and sexually transmitted diseases.

There are two very important things to know about contraceptives: *No method is 100% effective if you are having intercourse, and no single method is right for everyone.* The next few pages contain information on the advantages and the disadvantages of many forms of birth control. This information is provided to help you decide what form of contraception is best for you and your partner. While reading these pages, it might be helpful to keep the following questions in mind:

- How safe is the method?
- How effective is the method if I use it perfectly compared to if I use it but occasionally make some mistakes (called typical use)?
- Does the method provide any other benefits besides preventing pregnancy, like protection from sexually transmitted diseases (STDs), decreasing acne, or decreasing menstrual problems?
- How much does the method cost and can I afford it?
- Will this work for me?
- Will I use this method every time? (This is especially important, because leaving a method in your dresser drawer provides NO protection at all!)
- Do I want my partner to know I'm using this method?
- Do I want anyone else, like my family, friends or others to know I'm using this method?

Parents can be a wonderful resource to help you make decisions about choosing and using contraception. But not everyone wants to discuss their contraception decisions with their parents. It is important to know that you can buy over-the-counter or prescription contraception without your parents' permission (although it is a good idea to include them in these decisions when you can). If you feel you need to keep your reproductive health care private and confidential, there are family planning clinics in most locations (like Planned Parenthood or Family Health Council) where you can get free or inexpensive health care and contraception without your parents' involvement.

Not for Women Only!
You may notice that much of this section seems primarily addressed to women. That's because most birth control methods

are designed for women's bodies. Even the "male" methods work best when both partners – usually a man and a woman – know how to use them. Also, women are the ones who get pregnant.

But preventing pregnancy is still part of a guy's responsibility. Both guys and girls may find it helpful to discuss ahead of time what they would want the girl to do if she accidentally gets pregnant. If you two do not see eye to eye on what you would want to do about an unplanned pregnancy you might want to know that before you start having sex with each other. When a girl gets pregnant, she is the one that gets to make the final decision about what she wants to do about the pregnancy. The guy may not want her to have the baby but if she wants to have the baby, she can and there is nothing he can do about it. In the case of teenage pregnancy, when a teenager has a baby and applies for welfare, she is required by law to name the father. The father is then responsible for providing financial support to that child for the next 18 years. So guys, pay attention – contraception concerns you! A good way for a guy to show that he respects his partner and wants to protect her health, is to take some responsibility for the birth control they use. Guys can take responsibility in several ways by learning about different contraceptive options, helping their female partners remember to use their contraceptives methods, helping to pay for the method, and wearing male condoms.

Contraceptive Method Effectiveness
NOTE: The failure rates cited here are typical first year failure rates. The failure rate is the percent of women who get pregnant while using that type of birth control over the course of a year in the "real world." These percentages include women who use the contraception improperly (like forgetting to take the pill every day), which is why they reflect the "real world." This is also called *typical use*. For instance, the 8% typical use failure rate of birth control pills means that for every 100 women taking the pill, 8 will become pregnant in one year of having sex.

There is a second, lower failure rate cited for some methods, which is the *perfect use* failure rate. This is the percentage of women who use the birth control consistently and correctly every time they have sex (in other words, perfectly), but still get pregnant. For the pill, the perfect user failure rate is 0.3%, meaning that for every 1000 women who use the pill correctly and never forget to take a pill, three will get pregnant over the course of one year.

However, since none of us is perfect, you may want to base your choice of contraceptive method on the *typical use* failure rate. Generally, these higher failure percentages are more realistic. On this page is a table that can help you compare how well or badly each of these methods work to prevent pregnancy

Annual Pregnancy (Failure) Rates

	Typical Use	Perfect Use
Nothing	85%	85%
Vaginal Spermicide (gel, film, foam)	29%	15%
Withdrawal	27%	4%
Female Condom	21%	5%
Rhythm Method	20%	13%
Diaphragm or Cervical Cap	16%	6%
Contraceptive Sponge		
Never had a baby	16%	9%
Had a baby	32%	20%
Male Condom	15%	2%
Birth Control Pills	8%	0.3%
OrthoEvra® Patch	8%	0.3%
NuvaRing® (Vaginal Ring)	8%	0.3%
Depo-Provera® shot	3%	0.3%
ParaGard (Copper-T) IUD	0.1%	0.1%
Mirena® IUS (Intrauterine System)	0.1%	0.1%

Typical use: In the *real world*, the way most people use the method (condoms break or you forget to use one, you forget a pill, you forget to get a shot, your patch falls off, your ring slips out of the vagina, etc.).

Perfect use: In a *perfect world*, when the method is used 100% consistently and correctly every time (you NEVER forget a pill, you're NEVER late getting a shot, you ALWAYS use condoms correctly, your patch NEVER falls off, etc.).

Source: Trussell J. Contraceptive efficacy. In Hatcher RA, Trussell J, Stewart F, et al. Contraceptive Technology: Eighteenth Revised Edition. New York NY: Ardent Media, 2004.

Abstinence

Method: One definition of abstinence means not having vaginal (penis-in-vagina) intercourse to avoid pregnancy. In order for this method to be effective, the two individuals involved in a relationship must both agree to abstain. Another definition of abstinence is to avoid any sexual activity that you or your partner feel might lead to sexual intercourse. Abstinence is everyone's first method, because it is what you are doing before you start having sex, and also whenever you're not sexually active.

Effectiveness: If you are abstinent and don't have sexual intercourse, you cannot get pregnant. It is 100% effective in preventing pregnancy and the spread of STDs.

Availability: Abstinence is available anytime and anywhere, to anyone.

Cost: Abstinence is free.

Advantages: Abstinence...
   • Is free, safe, always available, and 100% effective.

Disadvantages: Abstinence...
   • May be a difficult method to always follow.

You might want to keep a back-up method on hand, such as condoms and emergency contraception, in case you decide to have intercourse. If you don't abstain and don't use contraception, you have an 85% chance of getting pregnant in one year. Abstinence is a safe and effective way of preventing pregnancy. Many couples find other ways of being sexual and are very happy without having sex.

A wonderful feeling

For the first time in my life I feel totally loved by someone. It is the most wonderful feeling in the world. Our relationship doesn't include intercourse, although we've discussed it. My boyfriend really pays attention to how I'm feeling and never pressures me. He makes me feel so special!

There are many reasons to abstain – you don't have a condom or are not using any other effective method to prevent pregnancy, you're not in the mood, or you don't like the person – but the decision to have or not to have intercourse is always up to you. You can make the decision to abstain from sex whenever you want.

Four Time Frames in Which to Think About Abstinence

1. Virginity - abstinence until marriage or until a long, long term relationship

Waiting until marriage can prevent so many complications from sexual intimacy and may be the approach an individual feels most comfortable with in terms of his or her spiritual journey.

2. Secondary Virginity - return to abstinence until marriage or until a long, long term relationship

A person can always choose to return to this long-term approach to abstinence. You always have the option even if you have had several partners.

3. Abstinence for a while
This could be until you are certain you are on an effective contraceptive, until both of you have been tested and are not infected with any sexually transmitted disease, or until your partner (or you) return home from a long, long trip.

4. Abstinence TONIGHT... TODAY... or NOW!

Each night about 10 million women who do not want to become pregnant have intercourse. Between 5% and 10% of those acts of intercourse — 500,000 to 1 million — are completely unprotected (no contraceptive). Abstinence today is what those 500,000 to 1 million women and men would be wise to use — TONIGHT!

Vaginal Spermicides
Foam, Suppository, Film, Jelly, Cream (vaginal spermicides)

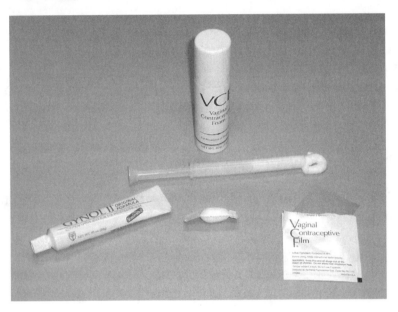

Method: Vaginal spermicidal foams, suppositories, films, jellies, and creams are all put into the vagina prior to intercourse. Spermicides have a chemical (usually nonoxnyl-9, also called N-9) that kills the guy's sperm by breaking down the sperm's cell walls. This is not the same thing as using a condom that is merely lubricated with a thin layer of spermicide (see Condom section). Wet vaginal spermicides like foam, cream, and jelly are put into the vagina with an applicator (kind of like a tampon applicator). When we say the word "cream" or "jelly" we don't mean the kind you eat! Those kinds may be yummy but they won't help you prevent pregnancy. Dry vaginal spermicides like vaginal contraceptive film (VCF) and suppositories are put into the vagina with your finger. Be sure that your spermicide is in place before the penis goes into the vagina. The dry methods (suppositories and films) need a few minutes to melt inside the vagina for them to work, so put them in the vagina 15 minutes before intercourse. Also, spermicides only last for about an hour, so you have to apply a new dose each time you have intercourse or if intercourse lasts longer than one hour.

Effectiveness: The typical first year failure rate is 29% for vaginal spermicides alone. The perfect user failure rate is 15%. Although they are not extremely effective when used alone, vaginal spermicides can add more protection when used with mechanical barriers like male or female condoms, diaphragms, or cervical caps. When used properly, Mechanical Barriers + Vaginal Spermicides = Better Protection!

Availability: Vaginal spermicides can be purchased at clinics and drug stores, and they do not require a prescription or permission from your parents.

Cost: Vaginal spermicides cost $0.50-$3.50 per use. Some health insurance companies will pay for spermicides if you have a prescription, so ask your health care provider about this!

Advantages: Vaginal spermicides...
- Are easy to find in stores and don't require a prescription.
- Can be used by a woman without her partner's help.
- Can provide extra protection if the condom breaks (but only if it was already in the vagina before the condom broke).
- Can provide extra lubrication during intercourse (so a condom may be less likely to break).

Disadvantages: Vaginal spermicides...
- Can cause skin irritation (although changing to another product may help).
- Might have an unpleasant taste or smell.
- Takes time to be effective, so sexual activity may be interrupted or delayed. Times vary, so read instructions carefully!
- Do not protect against STDs or HIV.

Safety: Some people are allergic to spermicides (specifically, the chemical nonoxyl-9). Also, studies have shown that women who use vaginal spermicide several times a day with different sexual partners may be more likely to get HIV than those who use non-spermicidal lubricants. This is because spermicides can irritate the vaginal walls, causing them to have open areas that allow the HIV infection to enter.

Withdrawal ("Pulling Out")

Method: Withdrawal usually means that the man takes his penis out of the woman's vagina before ejaculation. This is supposed to keep the semen and sperm out of the woman's body, so that it can't fertilize an egg or spread STDs. However, when a man is sexually excited and the penis is hard, semen can leak out of the penis before ejaculation, and this leakage can be enough to cause pregnancy and spread infection. The best way to use the withdrawal method is to wipe clean the tip of the penis before putting it into the vagina. When the man pulls out, he should direct his ejaculation away from the woman's genitals.

Effectiveness: The typical failure rate is 27%. If done correctly and consistently, the perfect user failure rate is 4%.

Availability, Cost, and Advantages: Withdrawal...
- Requires no devices, involves no chemicals.
- Is available in any situation, at no cost.

Disadvantages: Withdrawal...
- Is difficult to do correctly and consistently – it takes a lot of self-control for a man to pull out of the vagina at the sexual "peak time" of ejaculation.
- Is risky - semen may seep out of the penis before ejaculation, possibly exposing the partner to millions of sperm that can fertilize an egg.
- Provides NO protection against STDs.

It is a good idea to have a back-up method, such as a spermicide that can be put into the vagina if withdrawal is unsuccessful. (However, this is not as effective as having a spermicide in the vagina before ejaculation.) Or, even better, take emergency contraception. Even if withdrawal has a high typical failure rate, it is much better than using no contraception at all – and if practiced consistently and correctly, withdrawal can be successful at preventing pregnancy.

Rhythm Method ("Natural Family Planning or Calendar Method")

Method: The rhythm method involves calculating when you are most likely to get pregnant during your cycle, and then avoiding having sex around the time of ovulation. This method can be very difficult to do, especially for teens whose periods are often irregular. This method, when done correctly, involves several steps, such as checking your temperature first thing every morning with a special basal body thermometer (your temperature goes up when you ovulate), keeping a calendar of your periods, and checking the color and thickness of the mucus coming from your cervix (the discharge changes naturally at different times in the cycle).

Effectiveness: Typical failure rate is 20%. If done correctly and consistently, the perfect user failure rate for adults is 13%.

Availability, Cost, and Advantages: The rhythm method...
 • Requires no devices.
 • Involves no chemicals.
 • Involves no hormones.
 • Is accepted by many religions

Disadvantages: The rhythm method...
 • Is difficult to do correctly and consistently – it takes at least 3 months of monitoring your periods, temperature, and cervical mucus thickness to figure out your usual cycle and when you ovulate.
 • Requires a lot of self-control, since you must avoid having sex at times during the cycle when a woman is most interested in sex.
 • Is risky - semen may live in the vagina up to 7 days after sex, possibly exposing the woman to sperm that can fertilize an egg.
 • Provides NO protection against STDs.

This is not one of the methods of contraception recommended for teenagers; it is difficult for adolescents to track their periods and daily changes in temperature and cervical discharge because they often have irregular periods. Also, having sex around or during your period is not a guaranteed way to avoid getting pregnant, since sperm can live in the vagina for up to 7 days after ejaculation. If you have irregular periods, you might be fertile during the time the sperm is inside you.

Barrier Methods

The Female Condom

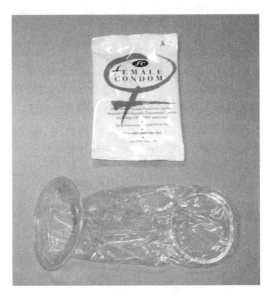

Method: The female condom is a long plastic pouch with a ring around the opening and a ring inside the pouch. A woman puts the pouch inside of her vagina, and, like the male condom, the female condom acts as a barrier to keep the sperm from getting inside to fertilize her egg. To use the female condom, first check the expiration date and check to make sure the package is completely sealed. Carefully open the package. Hold the condom with the open end down. Pinch the top inside ring between your thumb and second finger. Put the pinched ring and condom into the vagina, and push it in until you feel the pubic bone. Let go of the ring. Be sure to guide the guy's penis into the condom and not next to it. You want the penis inside the pouch so it does not touch the walls of the vagina. After sex, the guy should pull his penis out of the vagina but leave the female condom inside the vagina. Then twist the outside of the condom twice to make sure that the semen won't spill out, and gently pull the ring out of your vagina. Tie it in a knot and throw it away. Do not use the same condom again.

Effectiveness: Female condoms have a 21% typical user failure rate, and if used correctly the perfect failure rate is as low as a 5%.

Availability: You do not need a prescription or your parents' permission to buy female condoms. You can buy them at any drug store, some gas stations, and even in vending machines, although they may be harder to find than male condoms. Many family planning clinics give female condoms away for free.

Cost: $1.50 per female condom in drug stores, but they may be less expensive if you buy more at one time.

Advantages: The female condom...
- May be better for feeling the heat and the sensation of sex than the male condom.
- Is fairly effective at preventing pregnancy, and can reduce the spread of HIV and other STDs.
- Does not require a medical examination, prescription, or fitting before use.
- Gives the woman control over protecting her body from STDs and pregnancy.
- Can be inserted up to 8 hours before sex.
- Can be used by people who are allergic to latex, and by men who can't stay hard with male condoms.
- Can be combined with other methods, such as spermicides, the pill, patch, and Depo-Provera, to increase effectiveness. It should not be used together with other contraception methods that are put inside the vagina such as the diaphragm, cervical cap and vaginal ring.

Disadvantages: The female condom...
- May decrease sensitivity during intercourse, due to the extra layer between penis and vagina.
- May be difficult to use. Some people have trouble putting

the inside ring in place inside of the vagina. You need to feel comfortable touching your vagina, putting something in it before intercourse, and pulling something out of it after intercourse.
- Might be messy if the semen spills out of the condom.
- Might look unattractive or make a squeaking noise during sex (although extra lubricant can decrease the squeaking!).

Note: You cannot use a female condom and a male condom together at the same time because this will increase the chance that both will break. Overall, male condoms are safer than female condoms.

Diaphragm and Cervical Cap

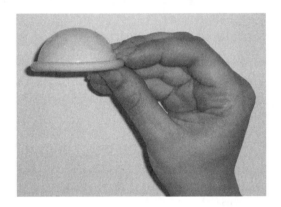

Method: Barrier methods, such as the diaphragm and cervical cap, are placed inside the vagina to cover the opening in the cervix that leads into the uterus. Most barrier methods work together with a vaginal spermicide, in the form of a jelly or cream, which kill sperm before they can fertilize the egg.
You must leave the diaphragm inside of your vagina for at least 6 hours after intercourse, and it can stay in for as long as 24 hours. You can leave a cervical cap inside for 48 hours. After this time period, both the diaphragm and the cervical cap can be washed, stored, and used again.

Effectiveness: The diaphragm and cervical cap's first year typical failure rate is 16%. The perfect failure rate for both is 6%. Since these barriers are meant to be used with spermicides, you should also study the spermicide failure rates.

Availability: You need to be fitted by a health care provider in order to buy a diaphragm or cervical cap, and you will need a prescription for it. You do not need parental permission to buy any of these methods.

Cost: Fitting for a cervical cap/diaphragm costs $50.00 - $100.00. The cost of a cervical cap/diaphragm with spermicide is $10.00 - $20.00.

Advantages: The diaphragm or cervical cap…
   • May add lubrication if used with a condom.
   • Is only used when needed.
   • Can be used by a woman without her partner's help.

Disadvantages: The diaphragm or cervical cap…
   • Requires consistent use (every time you have sex).
   • Can interrupt spontaneity.
   • Requires a visit to a health care provider for fitting.
   • Might be difficult to use. Putting the diaphragm or cervical cap in the vagina may be hard for some people. You need to feel comfortable touching your vagina, putting something in it before intercourse, and pulling something out of it several hours after intercourse.
   • Might be messy because of the required spermicide.

Safety: Generally, these two methods are safe. With all of them, however, there may be an increased risk of urinary tract and yeast infections. Both the diaphragm and cap can cause small cuts or openings on the cervix, although this usually means that it was not fitted properly. Lastly, some women are allergic to the latex and silicone used to make these barriers, or to the spermicides used with them. Once again – read the spermicide section, and be aware of your and your partner's allergies.

Contraceptive Sponge (Today® Sponge)

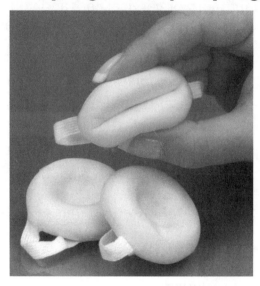

Method: The sponge is a circular polyurethane sponge that contains a spermicide (nonoxynol-9). It comes in one size. The concave dimple on one side of the sponge fits over the cervix. On the other side is a loop (strap) to make removal easier. The sponge is moistened with about 2 tablespoons of tap water prior to use and inserted into the vagina.

Effectiveness: The contraceptive sponge's first year typical and perfect use failure rates depend on whether or not a woman has had a baby; it is more effective for women who have never had a baby. The typical failure rate is 16% if a woman has never had a baby and 32% if she has had a baby. The perfect failure rate is 9% if a woman has never had a baby and 20% if she has had a baby.

Availability: Contraceptive sponge can be purchased at clinics, drug stores, and supermarkets. You do not need a prescription or permission from your parents to buy the sponge. The sponge can also be ordered over the internet by going to:
www.todaysponge.com
www.coolnurse.com/sponge.htm
www.womenshealth.about.com/cs/birthcontrol/a/todayspongebc.htm
www.blueskypharmacy.com/products/Sponges/116/

Cost: Contraceptive sponges cost about $3.00 per use. Some health insurance companies will pay for contraceptive sponge if you have a prescription, so ask your health care provider about this!

Advantages: Contraceptive sponges...
- Are sold over-the-counter and don't require a pelvic exam for fitting or a prescription. One size fits all women.
- Can be inserted in advance of sexual intercourse and remains effective for 24 hours no matter how many times a woman has intercourse.
- Do not interfere with normal activities, showers or baths.
- Can be used together with birth control pills, condoms, and most other methods to lower a woman's risk of pregnancy.
- Can provide extra protection if a condom breaks (but only if the sponge was already in the vagina before the condom broke).

Disdvantages: The contraceptive sponge...
- Requires consistent use (every time you have sex).
- Must be left in place for at least 6 hours after intercourse.
- Should not be worn longer than 24 to 30 hours - prolonged use may increase the risk for Toxic Shock Syndrome (TSS).
- Can cause skin irritation to the vagina or penis.
- Might be difficult to use. Putting the contraceptive sponge in the vagina may be hard for some people. You need to feel comfortable touching your vagina, putting something in it before intercourse, and pulling something out of it 6 hours after intercourse.
- Should not be used during a woman's menstrual periods.
- Does not protect against STDs or HIV.

Safety: Generally, the contraceptive sponge is safe. However, there may be an increased risk of urinary tract and yeast infections. Lastly, some women and men are allergic to nonoxynol-9, the spermicide in the contraceptive sponge. Read the spermicide section, and be aware of your and your partner's allergies.

The Male Condom

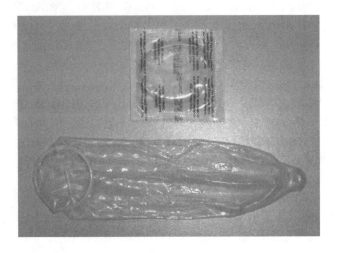

Methods: When a male condom is placed over the erect penis, it acts as a barrier that prevents sperm from entering the vagina. Some condoms are lubricated and some are coated with spermicide. Spermicidally-lubricated condoms (those that have nonoxynol-9) have no added benefit, in terms of pregnancy prevention, over other lubricated condoms; actually, they may cause irritation. However, a lubricated condom is preferred over a non-lubricated condom because it is less likely to break. If a condom is not lubricated, you can lubricate it yourself (inside and outside) with water, saliva, or one of many special condom lubricants, like K-Y® Jelly and Astroglide®. Never use Vaseline® or any oily products with a latex condom – they cause the rubber to break down and make the condom more likely to break (See page 58 for a list of safe and unsafe lubricants to use with latex condoms). There are three kinds of condoms: latex, polyurethane (a type of plastic), and natural lamb skin (made from animal's intestinal lining). All three types are very effective at preventing pregnancies, but the natural lamb skin condoms are not effective at preventing the transmission of two very important sexually transmitted diseases, HIV (human immunodeficiency virus) and Hepatitis B. Condoms come in many varieties, shapes, sizes, textures, and flavors. It can be fun to go to your local condom store and get a variety pack and find out which ones you and your partner like best!

Effectiveness: First year typical failure rates average about 15%. If used correctly and consistently, the failure rate falls to 2%. The condom's effectiveness depends heavily on how consistently you use it. Condoms break about 2% of the time – twice in approximately 100 acts of intercourse.

Availability: You do not need a prescription or your parents' permission to buy condoms. You can buy them at any drug store, some gas stations, and even in vending machines. Many family planning clinics and county health departments give condoms away for free.

Cost: $0.00 - $0.10 a piece in most family planning clinics, health departments, and university health services; $0.25 - $1.00 in drug stores. Polyurethane condoms cost about $1.00 - $1.50. Some health insurance companies will pay for condoms if you have a prescription, so ask your health care provider about this!

Advantages: The male condom...
- Is highly effective, and the best way (after abstinence) to decrease the spread of HIV and other STDs.
- Is cheap and readily available, and easy to carry around and use.
- Does not require a medical examination, prescription, or fitting before use.
- Gets men involved in contraception, which can make both partners more aware of the importance of protection.
- Can be combined with other methods, such as spermicides, diaphragms, the pill, the patch, the ring, or Depo-Provera®, to increase effectiveness.

Disadvantages: The male condom...
- Cannot be put on before the man has an erection (is hard), so the application process can interrupt spontaneity and sexual arousal.
- May decrease sensitivity during intercourse, due to the extra layer between penis and vagina.
- May irritate those with latex allergies (latex condoms only).
- Can only work when the man is willing to wear one.

- Natural lamb skin condoms DO NOT protect against HIV and other STDs.
- Polyurethane condoms are more expensive and have higher rates of breaking.

••

If your partner is stubborn about not wanting to wear a condom, try this:

Partner 1: *I love you! Would I give you an infection?*
Partner 2: Not on purpose, but many people don't know they're infected. That's why condoms are best for both of us.
1: *Just this once!*
2: Once is all it takes to get pregnant or infected.
1: *But using condoms is not romantic, and sex won't feel as good!*
2: We can work together to make it romantic and pleasurable. Besides, trust me: You definitely won't feel anything from me if we don't use a condom!

••

Safety: Condoms are completely safe for any couple not allergic to latex. If one of the two partners is truly allergic to latex, use a polyurethane condom instead.

Note: Never use two condoms at the same time to increase protection – they are less effective when worn this way. Air bubbles that form between the layers can burst, tearing holes in the condom.

Oral Contraceptives (Birth Control Pills)

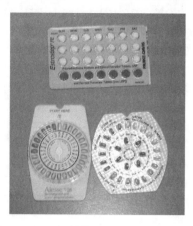

Method: Most birth control pills contain two types of hormones - estrogen and progestin. Some contain only progestin. These hormones mimic the natural effects of estrogen and progesterone that are made by the ovaries. Pills work mainly by preventing ovulation, and may also work by preventing the egg from implanting in the uterine lining. In order for this method to work, you must take one pill every day at roughly the same time (plus or minus 4 hours).

Effectiveness: The typical user failure rate for one year is 8%. Effectiveness depends on the user's ability to take a pill every day. If a woman takes the pill correctly and consistently (never missing a pill), the failure rate falls to 0.3%.

Availability: You must get a prescription for birth control pills from your health care provider and have check-ups to make sure you are not having any side effects from the pills. You can get pills without parental permission.

Cost: Birth control pills cost $0.00 - $10.00 per pack in family planning clinics and college health services, and $15.00 - $40.00 per pack in pharmacies if you pay cash. If you have a health insurance plan, the cost may be whatever your usual prescription drug co-pay is per month ($10.00 – $20.00).

Advantages: Birth control pills...
- Reduce the risks of cancer in the uterus and ovaries, as well as reduce the risk of fibroids in the uterus, benign breast cysts, ovarian cysts, and ectopic (tubal) pregnancies.
- Decrease menstrual cramps, menstrual blood loss, anemia, menstrual irregularities, and may decrease PMS. Pills are even more effective than prostaglandin inhibitors (like Advil®) at decreasing menstrual cramps!
- Reduce the risk of PID (pelvic inflammatory disease).
- Decrease acne and oily skin.
- Do not interrupt sex or foreplay.
- Can be used by a woman without her partner's help.

Disadvantages: Birth control pills...
- Have possible side effects such as mood changes, weight changes (usually less than 5 lbs up or down), breast fullness or tenderness, nausea, vomiting, blurred vision, spotting between periods or breakthrough bleeding, and decreased sex drive.
- May be hard to remember to use consistently– you must take a pill every day, at about the same time (plus or minus 4 hours).
- Provide NO protection against STDs, including HIV – so using a condom with the pill is a good idea).
- Have a small risk of causing blood clots (see Safety below for more details).

Safety: Today's birth control pills are very safe. There is very little evidence that birth control pills cause breast or cervical cancer. Pills do NOT hurt your ability to get pregnant after you stop taking them. Most pills today have a much lower dose of estrogen than several decades ago. If you have problems associated with heart disease (diabetes for more than 10 years, high blood pressure, high cholesterol), or have a personal or family history of blood clots in arteries or veins, you should consult a clinician before using birth control pills. Pills are not recommended for women who smoke cigarettes AND are over the age of 35; older women who smoke AND take the pill have a much higher risk of heart attacks and strokes. However, women under the age of 35 who smoke can still take the pill – but are highly encouraged to cut down on their smoking or stop before the age of 35. Pill users should be aware of the following symptoms of a blood clot, which spell the word "ACHES":

A – Abdominal pain (severe, not like a usual upset stomach)
C – Chest pain, shortness of breath or coughing up blood
H – Headaches (severe, not like a usual headache)
E – Eye problems, like blurred or loss of vision
S – Severe leg pain, swelling or purple color in the leg

If any of these symptoms occur, see a health care provider as soon as possible to make sure that you don't have a blood clot.

When to start the pill: Most teenagers think that a woman has to wait for the first day of her period to start her 1st pack of birth control pills. Others have heard that a woman should start her 1st pack of pills the Sunday after her next menstrual period. While these are both acceptable ways to start the pill today, more and more health care providers recommend that a woman start her first pack of birth control pills the day she gets the pack (called the Quick Start Method). The older ways of starting the pill may have resulted in many women getting pregnant while waiting to get their periods to start the pill!!

One advantage of the Quick Start Method is that you start taking the pills when you are most motivated to start which is right after you get them and the instructions are fresh in your mind. Another advantage of the Quick Start Method is that you get started sooner and are protected from pregnancy more quickly. When you start the first pack of pills at any time during your menstrual cycle other than your period, you will be protected from pregnancy after taking the first 7-10 days of the pill pack (as long as you do not miss or skip any pills).

For extra safety, many health care providers advise women to use a back up, like a condom, for the first 2 weeks of the 1st pill pack. However, if your condom breaks during the first 10-14 days of the 1st pack, you may want to get Emergency Contraception (See section called When Things Go Wrong). If you are going to be starting the pill, ask your health care provider about the Quick Start Method (starting it on the day you get the pills), rather than waiting until you get the next period.

Using the pill continuously: A woman who takes birth control pills does not need to stop taking them for monthly "rest periods" or after using it for an extended length of time. A woman can take the pill without a break for years, and when she is ready to get pregnant, all she needs to do is stop taking it. In fact, the Food and Drug Administration (FDA) recently approved a birth control pill called Seasonale® that is taken continuously (without 7 days of sugar or placebo pill every 28 days), so that a woman does not get a monthly period.

Seasonale® is designed so a woman takes 84 days of hormonally active pills followed by 7 days of sugar or placebo pills to make a 91 day cycle; a woman taking pills this way will get a period once a season (every 3 months) instead of approximately monthly (every 28 days). Other low dose pills can be taken in a similar way to safely skip the monthly period, as long as the hormonally active pills in the pack are all the same dose. To tell if a pack can be used this way, just look at the first 3 weeks of pills – if they are all the same color and shape, then they can be used continuously. However, it is a good idea to discuss this with your health care provider before doing it on your own.

There are a number of reasons why a woman might want to skip a monthly period. Some of them are medical reasons and some of them are for social convenience. Below are some common reasons why women might take birth control pills continuously to skip monthly periods:

Medical
- Severe menstrual symptoms like cramps, bloating, breast tenderness, headaches, heavy bleeding (despite taking pills in monthly cycles for 3 months)
- Ovarian cysts
- Anemia
- A hereditary or acquired bleeding condition like Von Willibrand's, hemophilia, low platelet count
- Any medical condition that gets worse during the period

Social
- Athletic, dance, or theatrical performances

- Travel or vacations
- Avoid cost of menstrual hygiene product
- Desire for fewer or no periods

Some health care providers believe that taking a pill continuously (skipping the 7 days of sugar or placebo pills every 28 days) may make the pill more effective and decrease the chance of break-through ovulation and pregnancy if a woman is late or misses a pill. Low dose pills can now be used without a break for 10 to 20 years.

The Patch (Ortho Evra®)

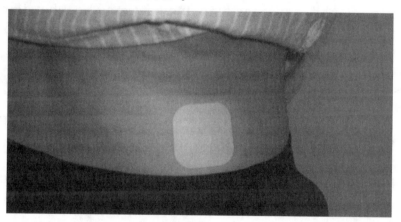

Method: Ortho Evra® is a 2-inch x 2-inch square beige-colored patch, similar to a big band-aid, that is worn on the upper outer arm, buttocks, abdomen, and upper torso (front or back but not on the breasts). The patch is worn on one body part for one week at a time, and then a new patch is put on a different body part weekly for three weeks. After three weeks, the patch is taken off for one week to allow a period.

The patch continuously releases estrogen and progestin hormones into the body through the skin, to stop ovulation. The patch has the same hormones found in some birth control pills. This cycle of three weeks of patch use (one patch a week) followed by one week of no patch use continues for as long as a woman wants birth control. Ortho Evra® is only effective if this cycle is followed, and if the patch is changed on the same day each week. It is important to rotate the places where the patch is worn to avoid skin irritation.

Effectiveness*: The typical first year failure rate is 8%, and the perfect user failure rate is 0.3%.

Availability: A health care provider needs to give you a prescription for the patch and should do check-ups to make sure the patch is not causing skin irritation or any other side effects.

Cost: Ortho Evra® patches may cost $30.00 - $40.00 per box of 3 patches (enough for a 28-day cycle) in pharmacies if you pay cash. Ortho Evra® may be cheaper at family planning clinics. If you have a health insurance plan, the cost may be whatever your usual prescription drug co-pay is per month ($10.00 - $20.00).

Advantages: Ortho Evra®...
- Is effective and easy to use.
- May be easier to remember to change a patch weekly than to take a daily pill.
- Can be used by a woman without her partner's help.
- Shortens and lightens blood flow during periods.
- Is reversible – if you want to get pregnant, simply stop using the patch.

Disadvantages: Ortho Evra®...
- May be seen by others, depending on where you wear it.
- May cause skin irritation, changes in the color of the skin under the patch, mood changes, minimal changes in weight, or breast tenderness.
- Requires the user to remember to change the patch every week on the same day, and to remember to restart the patch after the patch-free week.
- Occasionally the patch falls off. Although studies with adult women showed that patches fell off (partially or completely) only 5% of the time, studies with teen show this can happen more often (up to 30% of the time).
- Does not protect against STDs or HIV – so it is a good idea to use with a condom.
- Has a small risk of causing blood clots (see Safety below for more details).

- Is definitely less effective at preventing pregnancy for women who weigh 198 lbs or more; may be less effective for women who weigh between 175 and 198 lbs.

Safety: If you have problems associated with heart disease (diabetes for more than 10 years, high blood pressure, high cholesterol), or have a personal or family history of blood clots in arteries or veins, you should consult a health care provider before using Ortho Evra® patch. Ortho Evra® is not recommended for women who smoke cigarettes AND are over the age of 35; older women who smoke AND use the patch have a much higher risk of heart attacks and strokes. However, women under the age of 35 who smoke can still use the patch but are highly encouraged to cut down on their smoking or stop before the age of 35. Like pill users, patch users should be aware of the following symptoms of a blood clot, which spell the word "ACHES":

A – Abdominal pain (severe, not like a usual upset stomach)
C – Chest pain, shortness of breath or coughing up blood
H – Headaches (severe, not like a usual headache)
E – Eye problems, like blurred or loss of vision
S – Severe leg pain, swelling or purple color in the leg

If any of these symptoms occur, see a health care provider as soon as possible to make sure that you don't have a blood clot.

When to start the patch: Most teenagers think that a woman has to wait for the first day of her period to start her 1st patch. Others have heard that a woman should start her 1st patch the Sunday after her next menstrual period. These instructions delay you from starting the patch as soon as possible and can result in you getting pregnant while waiting to get your periods to start the patch!!

Today, more and more health care providers recommend that a woman start her first pack contraceptive patch the day she gets the 1st box of patches (this is called the Quick Start Method). One advantage of the Quick Start Method is that you start wearing the patch when you are most motivated to start which is right after you get the patch and the instructions are fresh in your mind.

Another advantage of the Quick Start Method is that you get started sooner and are protected from pregnancy more quickly.

When you start the first patch at any time during your menstrual cycle other than your period, you will be protected from pregnancy after wearing the first patch for 7 days (as long as that patch has not fallen off for more than 24 hours at any time during that 1st week).

For extra safety, health care providers advise women to use a back up, like a condom, during the first week of the 1st patch. However, if your condom breaks during the first 7 days of the 1st patch, you may want to get Emergency Contraception (See section called When Things Go Wrong). If you are going to be starting the patch, ask your health care provider about the Quick Start Method (starting it on the day you get the patch), rather than waiting until you get the next period.

Using the patch continuously: A woman who is using the patch can skip her periods by skipping the patch-free week by putting on a new patch for a week. There is less information on using the patch continuously (without a break) than on using pills continuously, but the same reasons why a woman might use the pill continuously could apply to a woman who uses the patch. Using the patch continuously (skipping the patch-free week) will be more expensive because you will need an extra 3 or 4 boxes of patches per year. It is a good idea to discuss continuous patch use with your health care provider before doing it on your own.

The Ring (NuvaRing®)

Method: NuvaRing® is a clear flexible silicone ring, about 2 inches across, which is put into the vagina and left in place for

3 weeks straight. The ring is then is taken out of the vagina for 1 week to allow a monthly period. At the end of each four-week cycle (three weeks with ring, one week without), a new ring is inserted and the cycle starts over. The ring slowly releases hormones (estrogen and progestin) through the vaginal wall, to prevent ovulation. The ring has similar hormones to some birth control pills.

Effectiveness: The typical first year failure rate of NuvaRing® is 8% (the same as the birth control pill and the patch). The perfect user failure rate is 0.3%.

Cost: NuvaRing® costs $30.00 - $40.00 per ring (enough for a 28-day cycle) in pharmacies if you pay cash. NuvaRing® may be cheaper at family planning clinics, if they provide it. If you have a health insurance plan, the cost may be whatever your usual prescription drug co-pay is per month ($10.00 - $20.00).

Advantages: NuvaRing®....
- Is discreet, effective, and easy to use.
- Only has to be put in the vagina once a month – which may be easier to remember compared to taking a pill every day or changing a patch every week.
- Can by used by a woman without her partner's help.

Disadvantages: NuvaRing®...
- Does not protect against STDs or HIV – so using it with a condom is a good idea.
- May cause an increase in vaginal discharge or vaginal irritation. However, the ring improves the natural, healthy bacteria in the vagina.
- Some women may consider putting the ring in the vagina to be difficult. You need to feel comfortable touching your vagina to put the ring in and take it out once a month.
- Has side effects similar to those of other hormonal contraceptives with estrogen and progestin (like the pill and the patch). These include spotting (light bleeding) between periods when you first start using it, minimal weight gain or loss, breast tenderness, and nausea.
- Has a small risk of causing blood clots (see Safety below for more details).

Safety: If you have problems associated with heart disease (diabetes for more than 10 years, high blood pressure, high cholesterol), or have a personal or family history of blood clots in arteries or veins, you should consult a health care provider before using NuvaRing®. NuvaRing® is not recommended for women who smoke cigarettes AND are over the age of 35; older women who smoke AND use the ring have a much higher risk of heart attacks and strokes. However, women under the age of 35 who smoke can still use the ring but are highly encouraged to cut down on their smoking or stop before the age of 35. Like pill and patch users, ring users should be aware of the following symptoms of a blood clot, which spell the word "ACHES":

A – Abdominal pain (severe, not like a usual upset stomach)
C – Chest pain, shortness of breath or coughing up blood
H – Headaches (severe, not like a usual headache)
E – Eye problems, like blurred or loss of vision
S – Severe leg pain, swelling or purple color in the leg

If any of these symptoms occur, see a health care provider as soon as possible to make sure that you don't have a blood clot.

When to start the ring: Most teenagers think that a woman has to wait for the first day of her period to put in her 1st ring. Others have heard that a woman should put in her 1st ring the Sunday after her next menstrual period. These instructions delay your starting the ring as soon as possible and can result in you getting pregnant while waiting to get your periods to start the ring!!

Today, more and more health care providers recommend that a woman put her first ring in the day she gets the 1st ring (this is called the Quick Start Method). One advantage of the Quick Start Method is that you start using the ring when you are most motivated to start which is right after you get the ring and the instructions are fresh in your mind. Another advantage of the Quick Start Method is that you get started sooner and are protected from pregnancy more quickly.

When you put in the 1st ring at any time during your menstrual cycle other than your period, you will be protected from pregnancy after wearing the 1st ring for 7 days (as long as that ring has not been taken out for more than 3 hours on any single day).

For extra safety, health care providers advise women to use a back up, like a condom, during the first week of the 1st ring. If your condom were to break during the first 7 days of using the 1st ring, you may want to get Emergency Contraception (See section called When Things Go Wrong). If you are going to be starting the ring, ask your health care provider about the Quick Start Method (starting it on the day you get the ring), rather than waiting until you get the next period.

Using the ring continuously: A woman who is using the ring can skip her periods by skipping the ring-free week and leaving the ring in for 4 weeks (instead of 3). At the end of the 4th week, she can then take out the old ring and put in a new ring for the next 4 weeks. The ring does not develop a bad odor when used for 3 or 4 weeks straight. Male partners rarely feel the ring and generally do not mind having sex with the ring in the woman's vagina. There is less information on using the ring continuously (without a 7 day break) than on using birth control pills continuously, but the same reasons why a woman might use the pill continuously could apply to a woman who uses the ring. Using the ring continuously (keeping it in the vagina for 4 weeks instead of 3 so you skip the ring-free week) does not cost any more than using it the way it was FDA-approved (3 weeks in and 1 week out). It is a good idea to discuss continuous ring use with your health care provider before doing it on your own.

Depo-Provera®
Method: Depo-Provera® is a progestin, a type of female sex hormone, which is given as a shot every three months. This hormone works to prevent pregnancy by stopping the egg from coming out of the ovary. It also thickens cervical mucus so sperm cannot enter the cervix, and thins the lining of the uterus so a fertilized egg cannot implant.

Effectiveness*: Depo-Provera® has a 3% typical user first year failure rate. The perfect user failure rate is 0.3%.

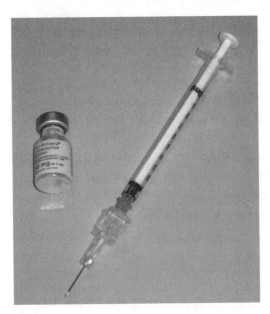

Availability: A health care provider needs to give an injection of Depo-Provera® in your arm or buttock muscle every three months and should do check ups to make sure you are not having any side effects from the shot. You can get Depo-Provera® shots without parental permission.

Cost: The cost ranges from $0.00 to $35.00 per injection. If you have a health insurance plan, the cost may be whatever your usual prescription drug co-pay is per month ($10.00 - $20.00).

Advantages: Depo-Provera®...
- Is a single 3 month-decision birth control – you don't have to remember to take any daily pills, remember to change a weekly patch, or deal with putting something into your vagina.
- Is long-lasting and extremely effective – for 3 months.
- Is reversible (if you stop getting your injections, your ability to have children will return within the next 9-18 months).
- Decreases menstrual flow (often over time stops menstrual periods) and decreases menstrual cramps and pain.
- Offers privacy (other people will not know you are using this birth control method unless you tell them).

Disadvantages: Depo-Provera®...
- Causes irregular menstrual cycles in most women, and increases the number of days of spotting and/or bleeding.

However, the longer you use it, the greater the likelihood that your periods will stop altogether (which some women like!).

- Delays return of fertility – on average, it takes 9-18 months to be able to get pregnant again. However, don't trust this as an extended form of contraception, since some teenagers get pregnant 14 weeks (3 months and 2 weeks) after their last shot.
- Provides no protection against STDs, including HIV – so use condoms to prevent yourself from getting infections.
- Requires regular (once every 3 months) visits to a clinic.
- Can cause a decrease in bone mineral density (loss of calcium in bones). The loss in calcium increases the longer Depo-Provera® is used. Some health care providers may recommend switching to another contraceptive method after 2 years of continuous use.

Safety: Depo-Provera® is considered a very safe contraceptive method for most women, including teenagers. However, recent concerns about the effect of Depo-Provera on bone health mean that any teenager using Depo-Provera should make sure she is doing all she can to protect her bones.

To develop and maintain healthy bones, she should do regular, weight-bearing physical activity for 20-30 minutes a day, at least 5 days a week. Second, she should make sure she gets 1200 - 1300 mg of calcium and adequate vitamin D each day. This can be done by eating foods and drinking beverages that have calcium, or by taking calcium supplements. Two calcium supplements that teenagers tend to like are Viactiv® Calcium Chews and Extra-Strength Tums®. Viactiv® is a soft, chewable candy-flavored cube the size of a caramel, which has 500 mg of calcium in each piece. That means that you only need to eat two or three per day to meet your daily requirement! Extra-Strength Tums® come in a variety of flavors, and each tablet provides 300 mg of calcium (They are less chalky if you suck on them instead of chewing them). Added to a healthy diet, either supplement allows you to meet your calcium needs easily!

On the next page is a list of foods and their calcium contents per serving, so you can properly plan to get 1200-1300 mg of calcium a day.

Calcium Counter

Figure out how you can get all the calcium you need in your diet!

Milk Group	Calcium
Plain nonfat yogurt, 1 cup	452 mg
Plain lowfat yogurt, 1 cup	415 mg
Swiss cheese, 1½ cup	408 mg
Chocolate milk shake, 10 ft oz	374 mg
American process cheese, 2 oz	348 mg
Fruit-flavored lowfat yogurt, 1 cup	345 mg
Mozzarella cheese (part skim) 1½ oz	311 mg
Cheddar cheese, 1½ oz	306 mg
Skim, nonfat, fat free milk, 1 cup	302 mg
1% lowfat milk, 1 cup	300 mg
2% reduced fat milk, 1 cup	297 mg
Whole milk, 1 cup	291 mg
1% lowfat chocolate milk, 1 cup	287 mg
2% reduced fat chocolate milk, 1 cup	284 mg
Chocolate milk, 1 cup	280 mg
Soft-serve ice cream, ½ cup	118 mg
Ice cream, 11% fat, ½ cup	88 mg
2% reduced fat cottage cheese, ½ cup	78 mg

Vegetable Group	Calcium
Frozen cooked kale, ½ cup	90 mg
Frozen cooked okra, ½ cup	88 mg
Frozen cooked beet greens, ½ cup	82 mg
Frozen cooked broccoli, ½ cup	47 mg

Meat Group	Calcium
Sardines with bones, 3 oz	371 mg
Canned salmon with bones, 3 oz	167 mg
Almonds, cup	120 mg

Fruit Group	Calcium
Orange juice, calcium fortified, 8 oz	300 mg
Orange, 1	52 mg

Grain Group	Calcium
Enriched English muffin, 1	96 mg
Pancakes, made with milk, 2	72 mg
Hamburger bun, 1	54 mg
Corn tortilla, 1	42 mg
Packet instant oatmeal, 1	19 mg

Combination Foods	Calcium
Baked potato with cheese, 1	350 mg
Taco salad, 1	280 mg
Cheese pizza, 1 slice	220 mg
Taco, 1 small	109 mg

Coffee Beverages	Calcium
Caffe latte, 12 fl oz	412 mg
Caffe mocha, 12 fl oz	337 mg
Cappuccino, 12 fl oz	262 mg

When to start Depo-Provera: Most teenagers think that a woman has to wait for the first day of her period to get in her 1st Depo-Provera shot. Others have heard that a woman should get her 1st shot within 5 days of her next menstrual period. Health care providers often prefer to give the first Depo-Provera shot within the first 5 days of the menstrual period to make sure a woman is not pregnant when getting the first shot. However, this can delay your starting Depo-Provera as soon as possible and can result in your getting pregnant while waiting to get your periods to start the shot!!

Today, more and more health care providers will give a woman her first Depo-Provera shot the day she comes in for her appointment, even if she is not menstruating, as long as she has not had any unprotected sex in the past 2 weeks and her pregnancy test is negative (this is called the Quick Start Method). One advantage of the Quick Start Method is that you get your first shot when you are most motivated to start which is the day of your appointment and you do not have to coordinate the first shot with the arrival of the next period. Another advantage of the Quick Start Method is that you get started sooner and are protected from pregnancy more quickly.

When you get your 1st shot at any time during your menstrual cycle other than your period, you will be protected from pregnancy 14 days after the first shot. For extra safety, health care providers advise women to use a back up, like a condom, during the first 2 week of getting the 1st shot. If your condom breaks during the first 2 weeks after getting the 1st shot, you may want to get Emergency Contraception (See section called When

Things Go Wrong, page 119). If you are going to be starting Depo-Provera, ask your health care provider about the Quick Start Method (getting the 1st shot on the day of your visit even if you are not having your period).

ParaGard® or Copper-T Intrauterine Device (IUD) and Mirena® Intrauterine System (IUS)

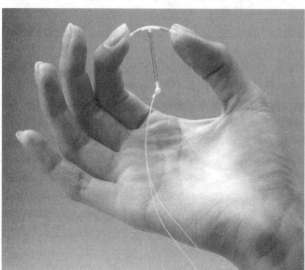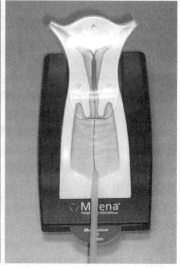

Method: Two IUDs are available in the United States; one is a non-hormonal type called the ParaGard® (or Copper-T) IUD, and the other is a hormonal type called the Mirena® IUS, which contains a progestin similar to many birth control pills. IUDs are small T-shaped plastic devices that are inserted into the uterus by a health care provider to provide long-term birth control.

The ParaGard® IUD is effective for ten years, while the Mirena® is effective for five years. The Copper-T or ParaGard® IUD works by preventing implantation of the egg or by preventing sperm from fertilizing the egg. The Mirena® works by releasing a hormone to thicken cervical mucus so sperm cannot enter the cervix and thins the lining of the uterus so a fertilized egg cannot implant.

A thread-like string hangs down from the IUD into the vagina from the cervix, which makes it easy for a health care provider to remove and check the position of the IUD. This string cannot be seen; you can only feel it if you put your finger into the vagina.

Effectiveness: ParaGard® IUD and Mirena® IUS are very effective! They have a typical user failure rate of less than 1% in the first year, and a perfect user failure rate of 0.1%.

Availability: A health care provider needs to put an IUD in and take it out of the uterus. Generally, IUDs have not been advised for teenagers or for women who have never been pregnant. However, this may be changing, so ask your health care provider about it.

Cost: The total cost of an IUD exam, insertion, and follow-up visit is $175.00 - $500.00.

Advantages: ParaGard® and Mirena®...
- Are discreet, easy to use, and extremely low-maintenance.
- Are very effective long-term methods of birth control.
- Can be used by a woman without her partner's help.
- Are reversible – in fact, IUDs are the most popular form of reversible contraception! Worldwide, 85 million women use them.
- The Mirena® may stop menstrual flow, and it reduces menstrual flow and cramps.

Disadvantages: ParaGard® and Mirena®...
- Have a high one-time cost, and many health care providers will not offer them to teenagers.
- Pose a slight risk of infection, especially in women with recent vaginal infections or more than one sexual partner.
- Do not protect against STDs or HIV.
- ParaGard® IUD may cause heavier periods and increased cramps.
- May come out without a woman realizing it, leaving her unprotected

Safety: Although the trend may be changing, for the past several decades IUDs have not generally been recommended for anyone who has not had children but would still like to. The most important serious complication of IUDs is infection. As a result, IUDs have not been considered ideal for women who have had an STD or Pelvic Inflammatory Disease (PID), women with multiple partners, and women whose partners have been sexually active with many other people. Occasionally (about 7% of the time), IUDs accidentally come out of the uterus and need to be put back in. To ensure protection, women with IUDs are told to check the IUD string regularly, and to use condoms for the first few months after IUD insertion. If you have an IUD, it is a good idea to get tested for STDs every 6 months and use condoms to prevent STDs.

Possible Future Methods

The Return of Hormonal Implants (Norplant® and Implanon®)

Method: Implants are soft plastic capsules containing a progestin hormone that is released over time. Norplant® was an FDA-approved implant that is no longer available in the U.S., although women in other countries can still get this contraceptive method. Norplant® is a progestin-only contraceptive method that consists of 6 flexible plastic rods containing a hormone similar to one in many birth control pills. These rods are implanted underneath the skin in the inside of the upper arm through a small cut in the skin. Norplant® provides extremely effective contraception for 5 years after the rods are inserted. Implants prevent pregnancy by causing the cervical mucus to thicken and by thinning the lining of the uterus to prevent implantation, and sometimes they stop ovulation. Although the first FDA-approved contraceptive implant, Norplant®, is no longer available in the U.S., another implant called Implanon® may soon be approved. Currently, no implants are available in the U.S.

Effectiveness*: Norplant® has a .09% typical user first year failure rate. In other words, only about one in 1000 women got pregnant in the first year of Norplant® use.

Safety: Norplant® is considered safe for most women, including teenagers. It is no longer available in the U.S. because of initial concerns that some of the rods were not working for the whole 5 years. Following an investigation, the company decided to stop marketing Norplant® in the U.S. because of financial concerns about being sued.

WHEN THINGS GO WRONG...

Some statistics to consider:
- In the U.S., close to 1 million teens become pregnant each year.
- Of these pregnancies, 85% are unplanned.
- Of these pregnancies, about almost one third end in abortion, one third end in spontaneous miscarriage, and one third are continued to term.

After sex you may be tired, or you may want to relax and enjoy your partner's company. But what if the condom broke? What if you didn't use anything to prevent pregnancy? What do you do when things go wrong? You can't relax just yet.

If your initial pregnancy prevention plan did not work, or you forgot to use it, then there is a possibility that you or your partner could become pregnant. If you're not ready to become a parent, you have to decide what to do next. There are several options.

The Planned Parenthood website has lots of information on these options; visit it at

www.plannedparenthood.org/health

Options After Unprotected Sex

Post-coital (after sex) methods for preventing pregnancy are often called "morning after" or "emergency contraception" methods, because women need to get treatment very soon after unprotected sex. There are three post-coital options:

Option 1: Emergency Contraception (EC)

EC is a high dose of birth control pills, in a pre-packaged prescription called Plan B®. You should consider taking EC pills any time sex is unprotected! Some common examples are when you have sex and:
- Your condom breaks or slips off during sex.
- You missed 2 or more pills in a row during the first three weeks of any pack of pills (only the placebo or sugar pills - usually the last 7 pills of the pack- can be safely missed).
- You are more than 2 days late starting a new pack of pills after the 7 days of sugar or placebo pills.

- Your patch falls off for more than 24 hours during the patch-on weeks.
- You are more than 2 days late putting a new patch on after the patch-free week.
- You left a single patch on for more than 9 days straight
- Your ring is out of the vagina for more than 3 hours during the 3 ring-in weeks.
- You are more than 2 days late putting a new ring in the vagina after the ring-out week.
- You left the ring in for more than 5 weeks in a row
- It has been more than 13 weeks since you got your last Depo-Provera® shot.
- You just started a new hormonal birth control method in the past 1-2 weeks, like Depo-Provera, the pill, the patch or the ring and did not use a back up or your back up failed.

You can get EC pills with a prescription from a health care provider. It is important that you take the pills within 120 hours (5 days) after unprotected sex, and the sooner you take them the more effective they are – so see your health care provider as soon as possible! If you have Plan B®, it is now recommended that you take the two white tablets together as soon as possible but no later than 120 hours after the last unprotected sex, rather than splitting the dose and taking one tablet now and another in 12 hours. When taken within the first 120 hours (5 days) of unprotected sex, EC can decrease the chance of your getting pregnant by 75-89%. The widespread use of emergency contraceptive pills could prevent one million abortions each year in the United States.

Many people ask "How does EC work? Is it a type of abortion?" Research to date shows that the main way EC works is to delay ovulation which prevents pregnancy. Another way it may work is to prevent a fertilized egg from sticking to the lining of the uterus. Once a fertilized egg is attached to the lining of the uterus a woman is pregnant and EC will no longer work or harm the pregnancy.

EC is not a type of abortion. Although some people believe that preventing a fertilized egg from sticking to the lining of the uterus is against their beliefs and they may not want to use EC for this reason. EC should not be confused with mifepristone (also called RU486 or the abortion pill).

One way of making sure you can get EC when you need it is to ask for the pills or a prescription to have at home. This will ensure that you have the fastest possible access to EC whenever necessary. Call your health care provider, a Planned Parenthood, or your hospital or family planning clinic to get a prescription for emergency contraceptive pills today!

Although Plan B® is now the preferred method of EC, sometimes it is not available. To find a list of which regular birth control pills can be used for EC and how many should be taken, go to www.arhp.org/ec (website of the Association of Reproductive Health Professionals) or www.not-2-late.com (website of Princeton University). Although taking a higher dose of certain regular birth control pills can be used for EC, these higher doses of regular birth control pills for EC are less effective at preventing pregnancy than Plan B®, and they may make you feel nauseous. This nausea is usually mild and should stop within a day or so, but many health care providers would recommend you take an over-the-counter anti-nausea pill, like Dramamine® or Bonine®, if you are going to be taking regular birth control pills for EC. If you vomit soon after taking the pills, you should contact your health care provider to see if you might need additional pills. Also, be aware that there may be other side effects from taking birth control pills. Other common temporary side effects include breast tenderness, cramps, fatigue, headaches, and irregular menstrual bleeding. For EC composed of higher doses of regular birth control pills, you should look for the same danger signs as when taking regular birth control pills. (See birth control pill section, page 101.)

If you were taking birth control pills, wearing the patch, or using the vaginal ring before having unprotected sex and you just took EC, you should restart your regular birth control method as soon as possible (that day or the next day). It is a good idea to get a pregnancy test 2 weeks after taking EC to make sure it worked. Remember that the method you just restarted may not protect you from pregnancy for 1-2 weeks so consider either not having sex for 2 weeks or use a back up, like a condom, if you do have sex.

If you were getting Depo-Provera shots but were late and you just took EC, it is safest to not have sex for 2 weeks and then go to your health care provider to get a pregnancy test 2 weeks after taking EC. If your pregnancy test is negative, you can get another Depo-Provera shot but remember you will not be protected from pregnancy for 2 more weeks after restarting the shot.

If you are not restarting a hormonal birth control method, your next menstrual period should begin within 3 weeks after taking EC. If it doesn't, see your health care provider for a pregnancy test. You may also want to consider having a pelvic exam 2 weeks after using EC to make sure that you did not get an STD.

Option 2: Insertion of IUD within 5 days of Unprotected Sex
Another form of emergency contraception is to insert an IUD into the woman's uterus after unprotected sex to reduce the chances of a fertilized egg attaching itself to the uterine lining. This post-coital method is very effective and the IUD is often left in place to provide future ongoing contraception. A trained health care provider can insert the IUD after an exam, but this method of emergency contraception is not recommended for teenagers and is very expensive. (See IUD section, page 116.)

Option 3: Wait and See
If your period is late, you should have a pregnancy test done. Home pregnancy tests can be bought at pharmacies and grocery stores without a prescription. These home tests are easy and private; however, they are not always accurate, so you should go to a clinic for a pregnancy test. If using a home pregnancy test, use your first morning urine for more accuracy. Tests can detect the pregnancy hormone (human chorionic gonadotropin – HCG) in your blood and urine 1 to 2 weeks after the fertilized egg attaches to the lining of the uterus. Early detection of pregnancy gives you more time to decide how you will handle it.

Dealing with an Unplanned Pregnancy

Making a decision about pregnancy can be especially difficult for teens, since they are not always psychologically or emotionally ready to make such a decision alone. One of the best ways you can help yourself to make a decision is to seek counseling. Talk to whomever you feel will be the most understanding, and who will have your best interests in mind. This could be your parents, an older sibling, your priest, rabbi, or minister, or a medical professional. Even with all this help, a final decision can be difficult to make. When an unplanned pregnancy happens, you and your partner need to decide whether or not to continue the pregnancy. The decision to have a child depends on many factors: financial resources, educational and career goals, relationships, religious values, and personal views. There are several options to consider.

Option 1: Continue the pregnancy and care for the child yourself

You may decide that even though you didn't plan to get pregnant, you want to have and raise a child. If this is the case, you need to arrange for prenatal care as soon as possible and start taking a prenatal vitamin with folic acid to prevent certain types of birth defects. Prenatal care is very important during all stages of pregnancy, but especially in the first three months.

Option 2: Continue the pregnancy and have the child adopted or placed in foster care

Although you may decide to continue the pregnancy, you might feel that you will be unable to care for the child after birth. If this is the case, it may be in your and your child's best interests to seek adoption or foster care. If this is the case, you should arrange for prenatal care as soon as possible and contact an adoption agency to explore your adoption choices.

Option 3: Terminate pregnancy (abortion)

Abortion is legal throughout the United States, but some states require parental permission or a meeting with a judge to obtain a court bypass, where the judge gives you permission for the abortion. In many states parental consent is not required, but counseling from your parents and other professional sources can still be helpful. Abortions done within the first 13 weeks of pregnancy are very safe and do not hurt your ability to get pregnant later when you are ready. Waiting longer than 13 weeks can increase the risk of abortion-related problems. If you decide to have an abortion, contact your health care provider or an abortion clinic to make plans. The sooner you decide, the safer the procedure.

Abortion can be a very emotional experience. The decision to have an abortion is not easy, and it should not be made hastily. Families and friends can be a helpful source of support, but it is the woman herself who must be comfortable with her decision.

••

I learned my lesson the hard way

At the age of 17, I unexpectedly got pregnant. I was devastated because I had planned to go to college, and I had so many things I wanted to do before settling down to have a family. My partner gave me so much support and encouragement. With his support, I was able to go through an abortion. Now I am on the pill, and I am still going with the same guy. Unfortunately, I learned my lesson the hard way, but it worked out fine. I am seriously taking precautions now and using contraception, so I won't get pregnant again until I'm ready.

••

Footnotes
* Much of the cases in this section and elsewhere in the book first appeared in <u>Sexual Etiquette 101 and Doctor, Am I a Virgin Again?</u> Special thanks, therefore to the individuals who did so much to develop and describe these rules of sexual etiquette. Deborah Cates, Shannon Dammann and Julie Convisser.

Part 3: Keeping Yourself Healthy

ALCOHOL AND YOU

Drinking alcohol when you are under age 21 is illegal. If you are caught drinking while underage, you may face severe penalties. Also, any person who is caught drinking and driving may be put in jail, be fined, or have his or her driver's license taken away. Adults who serve alcohol to minors or buy alcohol for them can also be punished.

Even though there are laws against it, teenagers still drink alcohol. When you are confronted with a situation where you need to make a decision about drinking alcohol, it is important to keep all these laws in mind. Drinking can lead to behaviors that you may later regret.

What actually happens to your body when you drink?

As you drink and the amount of alcohol in your bloodstream increases, many bodily changes occur:

- Your vision worsens
- Your ability to assess distances decreases
- Your pupils (the dark circular areas in the middle of your eyes) react more slowly to changes in light
- Your speech becomes slurred
- Your coordination decreases
- Your ability to solve problems is reduced
- Your emotions and moods become unpredictable
- Your judgment becomes poor

Although eating before drinking can slow the effects of alcohol on your body, nothing can stop the alcohol from eventually causing these changes. Once the alcohol is in your bloodstream, your body needs about 2 hours per drink to sober up.

Although drinking might seem like a fun way to have a good time, it can lead to dangerous situations. So, if you are going to drink, keep in mind some important rules:

1. **In the U.S., drinking alcohol is illegal under the age of 21.**
2. **If you have been drinking, don't drive.** Alcohol, even a small amount, can greatly reduce your ability to drive. More than half of all traffic deaths involve an intoxicated driver, and traffic death is the leading cause of teenage

death. Your driver's license will be taken away if you get caught drinking and driving. So, if you have been drinking, let somebody who has not been drinking drive. Better yet, before you go out, choose someone responsible to be a designated and sober driver.

3. **If you have to make any kind of important decisions, do not drink alcohol while or before deciding**. These decisions include sexual decisions. Alcohol weakens all judgment skills - including the ability to say "No" to sexual pressure. Be aware of anyone who tries to get you drunk – he or she is not looking out for your best interests.

4. **Avoid using alcohol as a problem-solver**. Many people try to cope with stress by drinking until they cannot remember their problems. Not only is this way of coping unhealthy for your body, but in the end, you are creating a new problem. If you find yourself drinking to run away from your problems, you may need help. (See the drinking quiz below.)

5. **You can say "No" whenever you want – whether it is before the first drink, or before the tenth**. Whenever you feel you have had enough, you should stop. Be in control of your alcohol intake. It may help to have two drinks without alcohol for every drink you have with alcohol, to help you keep better control over your drinking. It may also help to have just one drink and drink it slowly.

6. **Have a "buddy system" in place when you go out**. Have a friend watch your back (its better if he or she is not drinking) to make sure you don't drink too much and that you don't leave with anyone you don't know.

Alcoholism

People who are alcoholics have a disease that makes them unable to control their drinking. Very often, alcoholics need to drink regularly and in large quantities to feel satisfied. When you are under the influence of alcohol you may be reckless and lose control of your emotions and actions, but alcoholics are so dependent on the drink that their normal behavior is changed, too. Some signs of alcoholism include:

• Excessive alcohol consumption
• Making excuses to drink
• Needing to drink to feel good

- Depression (and its symptoms)
- Tremors (shaking)
- Changing behaviors (neglecting work, appearance, family)
- Changing mood

About 10 million Americans have alcohol-related problems, and some of them are quite young. **The following quiz* may help you decide if you have a drinking problem. Answer "Yes" or "No" to the following questions:**

1. Have you ever decided to stop drinking for a week or so, but only lasted a couple days?
2. Do you wish people would mind their own business about your drinking and stop telling you what to do?
3. Have you ever switched from one kind of drink to another in the hope that this would keep you from getting drunk?
4. Have you ever had a drink in the morning during the past year?
5. Do you envy people who can drink without getting into trouble?
6. Have you had problems connected with drinking during the past year?
7. Has your drinking caused trouble at home?
8. Do you ever try to get "extra" drinks at a party because you do not feel you get enough?
9. Do you tell yourself you can stop drinking at any time you want to, even though you keep getting drunk when you don't mean to?
10. Have you missed days of work or school because of drinking?
11. Do you have "blackouts?"
12. Have you ever felt that your life would be better if you did not drink?

Did you answer "Yes" 4 or more times? If so, you may have a problem with alcohol. You might find it helpful to look up Alcoholics Anonymous in the yellow pages and give them a call, or make an appointment with your health care provider to discuss it. Visit www.alcoholics-anonymous.org for more information.

Adolescents and Alcohol

Teenagers and college students are more likely than older adults to binge drink, which is an irregular drinking pattern marked by periods of heavy alcohol use separated by periods of very little or no alcohol use. For example, teenagers may go on drinking binges on weekends, at parties, or when upset, but stay relatively sober between binges. Binge drinking means drinking a certain number of drinks at one sitting. For men, drinking 5 or more drinks at a sitting is considered a binge; for women, 4 or more drinks is considered a binge. (The difference in the male and female numbers is due to the fact that women usually weigh less than men, and often have a lower tolerance for alcohol because of their lower weight.) This sort of irregular drinking can be very dangerous. You can easily lose of control of your actions and alcohol consumption, and an alcohol dependency may develop.

About one in six adolescents has a drinking problem, and about 7% of all teenagers are addicts (alcoholics). **The following CRAFFT test looks for alcohol problems in adolescents. Answer "Yes" or "No" to these six questions:**

C – Have you ever ridden in a *car* driven by someone (including yourself) who has been using alcohol?

R – Do you ever use alcohol to *relax*, feel better about yourself, or fit in?

A – Do you ever use alcohol while you are by yourself, *alone*?

F – Do you ever *forget* things you did while using alcohol

F – Do your family or *friends* ever tell you that you should cut down on your drinking?

T – Have you ever gotten into *trouble* while you were using alcohol?

If you said "Yes" 2 or more times, you probably have an alcohol problem. It may be helpful to call your health care provider or Alcoholics Anonymous for a more thorough assessment.

DRUGS AND YOU

What is a drug?
A drug is any chemical substance that produces physical, mental, emotional, or behavioral change in the person who uses it. Unfortunately, many drugs are widely available and easily abused. Sometimes people abuse prescription and legal drugs, but some illegal drugs are also commonly used. In the United States, young adults between 18 and 25 years old are the most likely group to abuse drugs. They usually get their first illegal drugs from their friends.

What happens to you when you take drugs?
Any mind-altering drug can impair your ability to make decisions, including choices about sex. Some drugs are "uppers" – they excite you and make you think you can do things you can't; some drugs are "downers" – they make you feel very mellow and sometimes depressed. If you are thinking about drugs, ask yourself if one high is worth the risk of addiction. If you are using illegal drugs, one bad decision that leads to addiction could put you at risk for a jail sentence. And with the use of any kind of drug, legal or illegal, you can seriously injure your brain, body, and relationships.

Drug Abuse
Drugs are abused by people of all backgrounds and ages. These substances include:

Legal
- Caffeine
- Alcohol (if you are 21 years old or older)
- Chewing tobacco and cigarettes (if you are 18 years or older)

Legal but can be misused and may be very dangerous
- Over the counter cold preparation (Nyquil, Coridcidin, Benadryl, cough syrups with dextromethorphan)
- Prescription narcotics (oxycontin, Demerol, Vicodan, Percocet, codeine, morphine, cocaine, fentanyl)
- Some anabolic steroids (usually used to enhance athletic performance, not to get high)
- Sedatives or "downers" (barbiturates, benzodiazepines)
- Hallucinogens (ketamine) — "special K"

- Stimulants or "uppers" (cocaine, amphetamines, Ritalin, diet pills),
- Inhalants (gases, glues, aerosols, paint thinner, hair spray)

Illegal
- Marijuana, "pot," or "weed"
- Narcotics (heroin)
- Some steroids (usually used to enhance athletic performance, not to get high)
- Hallucinogens (LSD, acid, mushrooms, PCP)
- Stimulants or "uppers" (crack, methamphetamines) — "crystal meth" or "ice"
- Club and date rape drugs (rohypnol or "roofies", ecstasy, GHB)

There are strict penalties for anyone caught making, buying, selling, or having these drugs in their possession. People can also become addicted to and abuse alcohol, cigarettes, and inhalants ("huffing" anything in a spray can, paint thinner, nail polish, permanent markers, and glue). Some of these can be legally bought in the U.S. (such as cigarettes at age 18 and alcohol at 21).

Tobacco and Nicotine
Nicotine and other additives are in cigarettes, cigars, and chewing tobacco. They may be legal (anyone over age 18 can buy them), but they can be very harmful to your health. About 25% of the U.S. population uses tobacco, and most smokers become addicted in their adolescent years. Smoking is highly addictive, very expensive as a life-long habit, and can cause lung cancer, heart disease, and stroke. According to the Center for the Advancement of Health, women who smoke tobacco double their chances of getting cancer of the cervix compared to non-smoking women. Smoking can also cause irregular menstrual periods and increase the risk or an ectopic or tubal pregnancy.

Marijuana
Marijuana, also called "pot" or "weed," is a popular illegal drug. Although possession, sale, purchase, and use of marijuana is illegal in all 50 states, about 49% of U.S. 12th graders have smoked a marijuana "joint." Marijuana is a mellowing drug – it impairs judgment, decreases motivation, and can hurt your short-

term memory. Like cigarettes, marijuana use is linked to cancer and heart disease; in fact, smoking three marijuana joints a week has the same health effects as smoking one pack of cigarettes a day! It is also expensive. Finally, marijuana is called a "gateway drug" because people who use it are much more likely to move on to using other, more dangerous illegal substances especially narcotics, stimulants, and hallucinogens. Marijuana can be laced with chemicals, crack, and other drugs, whether the users know it or not.

Smoking marijuana is not just unhealthy – it's risky! If you are going to smoke a joint, make sure you know where it's coming from, and that it's not laced with other dangerous drugs. Guys who smoke a lot of marijuana can develop gynecomastia (growth of breast tissue on the chest) and also may develop nipple discharge. The breast tissue growth may not go away on its own, even after a guy stops using marijuana.

Hallucinogens (mushrooms)
Psilocybin is a chemical found in some mushrooms, which people ingest (by eating raw, mixing with food, or brewing in tea) and call "mushrooms" or "shrooms." Hallucinogens like shrooms take users on "trips," where they experience very clear and intense hallucinations. This can last for 5-6 hours, and the effects are unpredictable. Even months after using the drug people can have flashbacks of their trips, so if a trip is bad, this can be a very unpleasant experience – long-term psychological problems can result. Physical effects include stomach pains, diarrhea, liver damage (if fake/laced mushrooms are used), and death (if overdose, or if wrong kind of mushroom used). Although shrooms are not addictive, users develop a tolerance and have to use more and more each time to experience the same intensity of effect. This is very dangerous, considering the unpredictability of the drug's effects.

Methylenedioxymethamphetimine (MDMA)
Street Names: *Ecstasy, E, X, XTC, Adam, Charity, Lover's Speed*

An amphetimine-based, hallucinogenic type drug that is taken orally, usually in a tablet or capsule form.

Effects:
- Lasts 3-6 hours
- Enables dancers to dance for long periods of time
- Incrases the chances of dehydration, hypertension, heart or kidney failure, and increased body temperature, which can lead to death
- Long-term effects include confusion, depression, sleep problems, anxiety, paranoia, and loss of memory

Gamma-hydoxybutyrate (GHB)
Street Names: *Grievous Bodily Harm, G, Liquid Ecstasy, Georgia Home Boy*

A central nervous system depressant that is usually ingested in liquid, powder, tablet, and capsule forms.

Effects:
- May last up to 4 hours, depending on the dose used
- Slows breathing and heart rates to dangerous levels
- Also has sedative and euphoric effects that begin up to 10-20 minutes from ingestion
- Use in connection with alcohol increases its potential for harm
- Overdose can occur quickly — sometimes death occurs

Methamphetamine
Street Names: *Speed, Ice, Chalk, Meth, Crystal, Crank, Fire, Glass*

A central nervous system stimulant, often found in pill, capsule, or powder form, whcih can be snorted, injected, or smoked.

Effects:
- Displays signs of agitation, excited speech, lack of appetite, and increased physical activity
- Often results in drastic weight loss, violence, psychotic behavior, paranoia, and sometimes damage to the heart or nervous system

Ketamine
Street Names: Special K, K, Vitamin K, Cat Valium

An injectable anesthetic used primarily by veteranarians, found either in liquid form or as a white powder that can be snorted or smoked, sometimes with marijuana.

Effects:
• Causes reactions similar to those of PCP, a hallucinatory drug
• Results in impaired attention, learning and memory function.
In larger doses, it may cause delirium, amnesia, impaired motor
function, high blood pressure, and depression

Rohypnol
Street Names: *Roofies, Rophies, Rcohe, Forget-Me Pill*

Tasteless and odorless sedative, easily soluble in carbonated
beverages, with toxic effects that are aggravated by concurrent
use of alcohol.

Effects:
• Can cause anterograde amnesia, which contributes to
Rohypnol's popularity as a "date rape" drug
• Can cause decreased blood pressure, drowsiness, visual
disturbances, dizziness, and confusion.

Lysergic Acid Diethylamide (LSD)
Street Names: *Acid, Boomers, Yellow Sunshines*

Hallucinogen that causes distortions in sensory perception,
usually taken orally either in tablet ot capsule form. Often sold on
blotter paper that has been saturated with the drug.

Effects:
• Are often unpredictable and may vary depending on dose,
enviroment, and the user
• Causes dilated pupils, higher body temperature, increased heart
rate and blood pressure, sweating, dry mouth, and tremors
• Can cause numbness, weakness and nausea
• Long-term effects may include persistent psychosis and
hallucinogenic persisting perception disorder, comonly known as
"flashbacks"

The Truth About Club Drugs

What are Raves?
"Raves" are high energy, all-night dances that feature hard pounding techno music and flashing laser lights. Raves are found in most metropolitan areas and, increasingly, in rural areas throughout the country. The parties are held in permanent dance clubs, abandoned warehouses, open fields, or empty buildings.

Raves are frequently advertised as "alcohol free" parties with hired security personnel. Internet sites often advertise these events as "safe" and "drug free." However, they are dangerously over-crowded parties where you can be exposed to rampant drug use and a high-crime environment. Numerous overdoses are documented at these events.

Raves are one of the most popular venues where club drugs are distributed. Club drugs include MDMA (more commonly known as "Ecstasy"), GHB and Rohypnol (also known as the "date rape" drugs), Ketamine, Methamphetamine (also known as "Meth" or "Ice"), and LSD.

Because some club drugs are colorless, odorless, and tasteless, they can be added without detection to beverages by individuals who want to intoxicate or sedate others in order to commit sexual assaults.

Rave promoters capitalize on the effects of club drugs. Bottled water and sports drinks are sold at Raves, often at inflated prices, to manage hyperthermia and dehydration. Also found are pacifiers to prevent involuntary teeth clenching, menthol nasal inhalers, surgical masks, chemical lights, and neon glow sticks to increase sensory perception and enhance the Rave experience.

Cool down rooms are provided, usually at a cost, as a place to cool off due to increased body temperature of the drug user.

Don't risk your health and safety. Tell your parents where you are going and consider asking them to come with you to the Rave site before you go by yourself.

Know the Signs

Effects of stimulant club drugs, such as MDMA and Methamphetamine:
- Increased heart rate
- Convulsions
- Extreme rise in body temperature
- Uncontrollable movements
- Insomnia
- Impaired speech
- Dehydration
- High blood pressure
- Grinding teeth

Effects of sedative/hallucinogenic club drugs, such as GHB, Ketamine, LSD and Rohypnol:
- Slow breathing
- Decreased heart rate (except LSD)
- Respiratory problems
- Intoxication
- Drowsiness
- Confusion
- Tremors
- Nausea

Effects common to all club drugs can include anxiety, panic, depression, euphoria, loss of memory, hallucinations, and psychotic behavior. Drugs, traces of drugs, and drug paraphernalia are direct evidence of drug abuse. Pacifiers, menthol inhalers, surgical masks, and other such items could also be considered indicators.

If you are knowingly using roofies or ecstasy, take precaution. Do not mix it with other drugs (like alcohol), drink plenty of fluids, and do not accept the drug from anyone you don't know and trust. To protect yourself from date rape: Keep your drink close, don't let anyone put something in your cup, and don't accept drinks from people you don't know and trust. If someone you know shows signs of being drugged, take him/her out of the area and seek immediate medical help.

Why do teenagers use drugs?

Everybody makes excuses or has reasons for why they do things they are not sure about. If you ask other teenagers why they use drugs, each one of them will probably come up with a different answer. Some reasons teenagers give for doing drugs include:

- To experiment
- To fit in with a group or peer pressure
- To satisfy their curiosity
- To escape from reality
- To solve a problem
- To get high or feel good or different
- Because of boredom
- In response to a dare
- To calm nerves or anxiety
- Because of addiction
- To feel less depressed
- To commit suicide
- Because drugs, especially alcohol and tobacco, are readily available
- Because they think that everybody is doing it
- To enhance sexual pleasure

Curiosity is certainly one reason for trying drugs. Experimentation with drugs is common among adolescents, but even if you're only trying a drug once, this can be very dangerous. Drug experimentation can lead to addiction – when you, your actions, and your moods are dependent on the drug. Even when they're not "high," drug addicts are thinking about and craving the drug. In short, addiction means that you cannot function normally, both with and without the drug in your body.

Once again, the CRAFFT test is specifically designed to identify drug abuse problems in adolescents.

Answer "Yes" or "No" to these six questions:

C – Have you ever ridden in a *car* driven by someone (including yourself) who was "high" or had been using drugs?

R – Do you ever use drugs to *relax*, feel better about yourself, or fit in?

A – Do you ever use drugs while you are by yourself, *alone*?

F – Do you ever *forget* things you did while using drugs?

F – Do your family or *friends* ever tell you that you should cut down on your drug use?

T – Have you ever gotten into *trouble* while you were using drugs?

If you answered "Yes" to 2 or more of the questions, you may have a problem with drugs. It might be a good idea to make an appointment to discuss this with your health care provider, or call Narcotics Anonymous (website www.na.org). Remember: The law will not punish you if you seek medical help for a drug addiction, so act now!

Things I Wouldn't Even Consider...
Remember the "Things I Wouldn't Even Consider..." list you made earlier in the book on page 75 and 76? The topic of that list included things you would never do in a sexual situation. It's also a good idea to decide on things you would never do in a non-sexual situation. Here are some examples from other people your age...

They said they wouldn't even consider...
   ...jumping on the bandwagon
   ...using physical strength or power to get someone to do what you want
   ...driving drunk
   ...not graduating high school
   ...discriminating against others
   ...being judgmental
   ...cheating in school
   ...defining themselves solely through others' eyes
   ...taking something that doesn't belong to them

Think about some non-sexual things that you would never want to do, and add them to your previous "Things I Wouldn't Even Consider..." list on page 75 and 76.

SEXUAL ABUSE, SEXUAL ASSAULT, AND RAPE

Sexual assault is a crime that includes forced sexual contact, ranging from kissing and fondling to sexual intercourse. Forced sexual contact happens to both girls and guys, and it is estimated that 1 in 8 high school students is involved in a violent relationship. It is important that you notice and report this violence, because a lot of violent relationships have the potential to lead to accidental deaths. Sexual abuse does not have to be physically violent; obscene phone calls and pornography are not physically violent, but they can be forms of sexual abuse. Teens with low self-esteem and/or violent childhood experiences at home are more likely to become easy targets for people who are looking for someone to abuse. Sexual abuse and assault can happen to anyone and by anyone, whether it be a complete stranger or someone you know very well.

In our society, people might be afraid to speak out about being forced into an unwanted sexual act unless there is physical proof of force. Often there is no proof, but this does not mean that force was not used. A person who is raped does not "ask for it" or cause it to happen in any way. Sexual assault has nothing to do with sexual desire, intimacy, or love; sexual assault is an act of violence and aggression driven by a lust for power, control, and dominance. Whether a person uses brutal force, drugs, alcohol, or verbal threats, or if the victim fights, screams, or silently submits, sexual violence is a crime and a violation of human rights.

Rape

Sexual assault, abuse, and rape are most likely to be committed by someone the victim knows. When a woman or a man is forced to have sex against her or his will on a date or by someone they are in a relationship with, it is called date rape. Date rape is a serious threat facing young people today, and it can occur in various places: not just on a date, but also often in places such as bars and clubs or at school or peoples' homes. Sometimes in date rape, one person uses a drug to sedate or disorient the person they plan to rape. Drugs can be put into any drink that is left unattended; one very popular date rape drug is called Rohypnol or roofies. Some of the many date rape drugs can cause brain damage and other serious problems for the person who is drugged. For all these reasons, it is so important to be aware and cautious - date rape can happen to anyone when they're not paying attention. According to the Pittsburgh Coalition Against Rape:

- 83% of girls and 79% of boys have been sexual harassed in high school;
- 1 out of every 4 girls and 1 out of every 6 boys are victims of sexual assault before the age of 18;
- 44% of people with disabilities will be raped by an employer;
- 95% of known perpetrators sexually abuse female children and 80% abuse male children;
- 302,091 women are rape

Many people think date rape has to involve violence or force but you can be legally charged with rape if you have sex with someone who is under the influence of alcohol and/or drugs. When one or both people are under the influence of alcohol and/or drugs, they might not be able to make a clear decision about having sex. Sex under the influence is not considered legally consensual (agreed by both parties who are able-minded). Even if someone agrees to have sex, seems to enjoy it and does not protest or say no, you still may have committed rape. Sex should be something you do when you have a clear head.

The long-term effects of sexual abuse and sexual assault (whether it is rape, incest, sexual violence, harassment, coercion, molestation, or any other kind of unwanted contact) can be very devastating. There is no reason why anyone should have to have sex when he or she does not want to. No one – not a father, mother, brother, sister, aunt, uncle, boyfriend, girlfriend, husband, wife, grandfather, grandmother, baby-sitter, or stranger – has the right to sexually abuse or violate another person's body.

It does not matter if you were wearing something sexy, or if you were taken out to an expensive dinner. You never owe someone sex. NEVER!

Survivors of sexual assault, whether they were victims as children or as adults, may suffer many of the same acute symptoms and long-term effects. If you have been assaulted in any way, you should get medical care. The following symptoms are warning signs that you, or someone you know, may need some help.

Symptoms of sexual assault include:
- overall soreness
- soreness and bruising in the area of the body that was the focus of the assault
- tension headaches
- fatigue and/or irritability
- weight gain or loss
- stomach pains, nausea, or loss of appetite
- pregnancy and/or sexually transmitted disease
- shock
- loss of control or feeling powerless
- denial and/or fear
- guilt, self blame, and/or depression
- sleep disturbances/nightmares
- fear of intimacy and inability to trust
- pain or burning in the genitals or during urination
- pain during subsequent sex
- anger
- memory loss (sense of "blacking out")
- flashbacks

In cases of sexual assault and sexual abuse, in addition to looking for physical and psychological scars, your health care provider may help you to deal with the possibility of pregnancy and the risk of sexually transmitted diseases (STDs).

What do you say to someone who you know has been raped? Below are a few suggested from Pittsburgh Action Against Rape (PAAR).

What to say to Someone Who Has Experienced Sexual Violence:
- I believe you and I'm glad you told me.
- I am really sorry that happened to you. I want you to know that it was not your fault

- It really took a lot of courage to talk about that.
- That must have been terrifying when…

You can learn about ways to prevent sexual assault and practice personal safety techniques through resources published by specialized agencies such as The National Committee for Prevention of Child Abuse, Battered Women, Incest Survivors Network, National Resource Center on Child Sexual Abuse, and Rape Crisis Centers. Many people can and do survive sexual assault and abuse, and many places provide help. You can check your phone book for local numbers, or call the hotline numbers listed in the back of this book.

The Rape, Abuse & Incest National Network - National Sexual Assault Hotline
1-800-656-HOPE
http://www.rainn.org

Sexual Assault Hotlines in the U.S. from The Feminist Majority Foundation's web site.
Local addresses and phone numbers for every state.
http://www.feminist.org/911/resources.html

National Child Abuse Hotline
To learn the reporting agency for your geographic area and situation.
1-800-4-A-CHILD (1-800-422-4453)
http://www.childhelpusa.org/

National Domestic Violence Hotline
1-800-799-SAFE (7233)

National Runaway Switchboard
1-800-621-4000

Girls and Boys Town
A national hotline that girls and boys can call with any problem at any time
1-800-448-3000; Hearing Impaired: 1-800-448-1833
http://www.girlsandboystown.org/home.asp

Parents Anonymous
Self help groups for abused children and parents under stress
1-800-421-0353
http://www.parentsanonymous.org/

Sexual Assault Hotline
1-800-656-4673

Stop It Now! (Sexual Abuse)
1-888-PREVENT
http://www.stopitnow.com/

United Way Crisis Helpline
1-800-233-HELP (1-800-233-4357)

AIDS AND OTHER SEXUALLY TRANSMITTED DISEASES (STDs)

The term sexually transmitted disease (STD) is used to describe over twenty different infections that are usually passed from one person to another person by sexual contact. Sexual contact does not only mean intercourse. Some infections can be passed from person to person by skin-to-skin contact, by hand to genital contact, by oral and by anal sex. Sexually transmitted infections may cause trouble in any part of the body that has been touched. And some STDs can affect the whole body.

STDs are more common and severe now than in the past. In addition to the more familiar bacterial infections (such as gonorrhea, syphilis and chlamydia), viral infections have increased dramatically. And then there are the parasitic infections like pubic lice and trichomonas. The most common sexually transmitted viral infections are known as the four H-viruses. They may be transmitted through sex and last a person's entire life. The H-viruses are:
 • human immunodeficiency virus (HIV)
 • herpes simplex virus (HSV)
 • hepatitis B virus (HBV)
 • human papilloma virus, including genital warts (HPV)

No cure exists for these infections caused by viruses. In the case of HIV, the infection can lead to failure of your immune system, which is called acquired immune deficiency syndrome (AIDS). Despite recent advances in developing new treatments, many people still die from AIDS.

Preventing the spread of infection is the best way to reduce the risk of spreading STDs. In general, the things you can do to protect yourself from HIV will also protect you from gonorrhea, Chlamydia, trichomonas, herpes, genital warts, and other STDs. Here are several things you can do to protect yourself from STDs. Some people call these the A, B, C's of preventing STDs:

- Abstain from all sexual activity with another person.
- Be sexually intimate with only one person, who is only sexually intimate with you (this is called mutual monogamy). This works when both of you are known to be uninfected, and when trusting each other to be faithful is realistic and practical.
- Be sexually intimate only when latex Condoms, dental dams, rubber gloves, or other barriers are used to prevent exchange of semen, blood, and vaginal secretions (a lubricant may be beneficial at the time of sex).
- Abstain from all sexual activities that could possibly result in the exchange of infected body fluids (such as blood, vaginal fluid, semen, and saliva) including vaginal, anal and oral intercourse, and also abstain from wet kissing when lips, gums, or other tissues are raw, bleeding, or have sores
- Do not share injection equipment or needles of any kind, including piercing and tattoo needles and even tooth brushes.

You may feel embarrassed or scared if you think you have been exposed to an STD, but asking for information and getting treatment is better than worrying and getting sicker, or passing it on to someone else. It is also extremely important that you talk to your partner about STDs and get sexual histories. Even if it is uncomfortable to do, it can save your life. In some cases it can even improve your relationship, as in the following case.

•••

Excellent communication about herpes

I fell in love with a girl, and just prior to having intercourse, she told me she had herpes (on the outer lips of her vagina). We did not have intercourse that night. Later, as we grew closer, I came to trust her. We decided that we could cooperate in taking precautions to prevent me from getting herpes. We used condoms every time. We had a beautiful relationship, and I never got infected. Her condition actually made our relationship deeper and closer because we communicated about it before we had sex the first time, so we trusted and cooperated with each other.

•••

If you are not comfortable enough with your partner to talk about STDs, you should not be having sex.

•••

I don't know him well enough to ask or to look!

A patient in a clinic had herpes and genital warts. When asked if her partner had any warts or lesions she replied, "I don't know him well enough to look.*" If you are going to have sex, you should be comfortable enough with your partner to ask about/ look for signs of STDs, and then take the necessary precautions. If this seems too personal, then maybe it's not time for sex!

*Most infections are asymptomatic. This means you can't see any signs of STDs. Always ask!

•••

Sexually Transmitted Diseases (STDs)
The following section briefly explains some of the more common sexually transmitted diseases and their possible symptoms, treatments (if available), and consequences if left untreated.

Be aware that you may have a STD without having any symptoms. It is important to have yourself checked out if you are afraid you may have caught something, or if you just want to know that everything is okay. You can even bring your partner along for an exam. Remember, whether it's the person you picked up at a party, or your next door neighbor, anyone can carry a STD. As the next case shows, image and reputation guarantee nothing about a person's disease status.

● ●

STDs from "wholesome" dates

A 14-year old patient went to get checked for vaginal discharge. Tests showed that she had gonorrhea, chlamydia, trich, bacterial vaginosis, and yeast. She was also pregnant. Surprised, she said her mother had always hand-picked the "wholesome" boys with whom she was allowed to socialize.

● ●

Even after you find out both you and your partner are infection-free, it is a good idea to always use a condom if you have intercourse.

● ●

She's HIV positive, and she's my sister

I am personally extremely careful about getting STDs. My sister exchanged sex for drugs in the past and is now HIV positive. I see what she is going through and I care too much to do that to myself or anyone else.

● ●

1. Human Immunodeficiency Virus (HIV) and Acquired Immune Deficiency Syndrome (AIDS)
When HIV has infected a person's blood, the virus attacks the

human T-lymphocytes, cells which normally protect people from infection and cancer. Usually an infected person has no symptoms at first, but over the years symptoms become increasingly severe as the immune system gradually weakens. The average time from getting HIV infection to the onset of AIDS (acquired immune deficiency syndrome) is about 10 years. There are many new treatments for HIV, like anti-retroviral medications and protease inhibitors, that can keep people with HIV healthy and alive for longer. Right now there is no known cure for this disease. Researchers are constantly looking for possible vaccines to prevent people from getting it and cures for people who already have the disease. However, early diagnosis and treatment of HIV can keep an infected person healthier and alive until there is a cure.

HIV testing is usually available, anonymously or confidentially, at STD clinics or other health clinics in your area. There are also over-the-counter blood and saliva tests for HIV, that you can buy and mail out for testing. (You call the testing company later for your results.)

HIV is transmitted by direct contact with body fluids rich in T-4 lymphocytes, such as blood, semen, and vaginal fluid. The virus probably cannot cross unbroken skin, but the skin in the mouth, vagina, rectum, urethra, cervix and endometrium can allow the virus to enter the body. Besides abstinence, using a condom is the best way to protect yourself. HIV CANNOT be transmitted through casual contact such as:
- shaking hands, hugging, dry kissing (with no exchange of saliva), sneezing, or coughing
- swimming in a pool with a person who is HIV infected
- sharing cleaned eating and drinking utensils
- sharing toilets, bathrooms, or kitchens

HIV is usually passed from person to person through sexual contact or infected needles. If you have ever done any one of the following, you should consider being tested for the virus:

Sexual Contacts
Have you ever had sex with...
   ...a man who has sex with men?
   ...a man who has sex with men and with women?
   ...a person you thought or knew was infected with HIV?
Have you ever had...
   ...a sexually transmitted disease such as gonorrhea,
      chlamydia, trichomonas, syphilis, herpes, or genital warts?
   ...more than 5 sex partners?
   ...sex without latex condoms?
   ...sex with someone who has or has had more than 5 sexual
      partners?

Drug Activities
Have you ever...
   ...used drugs using a needle or shared injection equipment?
   ...had sex with a person who uses or used needle drugs and
      shared injection equipment?

•••

Glad they kept in touch

*I used to think that AIDS was a distant problem that didn't
concern me personally. Then my partner's old girlfriend got in
touch with him to say that she had tested positive for HIV. It was
scary for both of us to hear. But I'm glad I know, so that now I
can make the right decisions and be aware. I'm truly grateful
she cared and let my boyfriend know. We are going to get tested
tomorrow.*

•••

HIV used to be diagnosed mostly by a blood test, but more
recently there are rapid saliva tests that can give your health
care provider the results within a half an hour. In addition, as
mentioned previously, there are mail-away tests for HIV that use
either blood or saliva.

Symptoms: After a person is infected, he or she may experience no symptoms early on. This asymptomatic stage may last for several years. Symptoms, when they do occur, include:
- chronic unexplained fatigue (tiredness)
- unexplained weight loss
- persistent diarrhea
- changes in mental state

Treatment: There is currently no cure for AIDS, which eventually leads to death. However, HIV can be treated (but not eliminated) with a number of different drugs like anti-retrovirals and protease inhibitors.

Most young men and women who are infected have no symptoms and do not know that they are infected. Since there is currently no cure for HIV infection and AIDS, people can best protect themselves by becoming educated about HIV transmission and learning to practice safer sex.

2. Chlamydia (cla – MIH – dee - ah)

Chlamydia is an infection caused by the bacteria chlamydia trachomatis. It is the most common bacterial STD in the United States, with 4 million new cases each year. It is especially common among teenagers and young adults. It frequently occurs together with gonorrhea infections (one-fourth of men and two-fifths of women who have gonorrhea also have chlamydia). Chlamydia is usually diagnosed by a urine test or by a cotton swab from the cervix in a woman or the urethra in a man.

Symptoms: Chlamydia symptoms may not appear for long periods of time, or may never appear - 75% of infected women and 50% of infected men do not know that they have it. When people have symptoms, they are different for men compared to women:
- **men** – painful burning sensation during urination, watery or clear mucus-like discharge from the penis,
- **women** – abnormal vaginal discharge, irregular vaginal bleeding or spotting, pelvic pain that may be accompanied by nausea and fever, painful or frequent urination.

Women are less likely to have symptoms. Therefore, it is

important to have chlamydia tests done during annual pelvic exams, whether or not you think you are infected. If you have ever had chlamydia, you should get re-tested for it every 6 months, whenever you have a new partner and have unprotected sex, or if you have any symptoms.

Treatment: Antibiotics such as a 7-day course of doxycycline or a single dose of azithromycin.

If Untreated: Women can develop pelvic inflammatory disease (PID) and other infections that can lead to infertility (an inability to get pregnant), chronic pelvic pain, or ectopic (tubal) pregnancy.

3. Gonorrhea (gone – o - RHEE - a)

Gonorrhea is a bacterial infection caused by Neisseria gonorrhea. This bacteria may cause infections of the urethra, bladder, prostate, epididymis, cervix, endometrium, fallopian tubes, throat, and other body parts such as blood, joints and skin. Gonorrhea is usually diagnosed by a urine test or by a cotton swab from the cervix of a woman or the urethra in a man.

Symptoms: Less dramatic symptoms in women, symptoms often seen in men:
- **men** – burning sensation during urination, yellow-green discharge from the penis, fever, painful sex,
- **women** – pain in pelvic area or back, unusual vaginal bleeding or spotting, bleeding after sex, yellow vaginal discharge, burning with urination, fever, severe menstrual cramps.

Treatment: Antibiotics such as ciprofloxacin (Cipro), cefixime (Suprax), or a shot of ceftriaxone (Rocephin). Some gonorrhea has become resistant to antibiotics such as ciprofloxacin, especially among people who live on the West Coast, in the South Pacific, or in Southeast Asia.

If Untreated: For women, if the infection reaches the fallopian tubes, there is a risk of scarring, tubal blockage and infertility (inability to get pregnant). The longer gonorrhea is left untreated and the greater the number of times the tubes are infected, the greater the chances of permanent damage.

4. Herpes Simplex (Her - pees - Sim - plex) Virus (HSV)

Herpes is a chronic virus that stays in a person's body for life. There are two types of herpes viruses: type I and type II. Type I is more likely to cause infections of the mouth but may be passed to the genitals through oral-genital contact. Type II is more likely to cause genital infections but may cause infections of the mouth as well. Herpes is usually diagnosed by rubbing a cotton swab on an open sore and sending it for a herpes culture.

••

I didn't want herpes, so I said "No"

I met a girl who I really liked, and we wanted to have sex. When she told me that she had herpes but was taking medication for it, I was shocked and refused to have sex with her. She didn't mind because she understood, and we talked about it. I asked my doctor if I could have caught it from her and he said it was unlikely. I am glad she told me about it before we had sex, so I had a choice.

••

Herpes hurts!

The first time I had sex with this one guy, I caught herpes. I have never been in so much pain in my life. I cried every time I went to the bathroom. I couldn't believe I had been stupid enough to have unprotected sex.

••

Symptoms: Extremely painful blisters (lesions) on the vulva, penis, or around the anus; tingling sensation prior to breaking out, fever (with the first outbreak), swollen glands in the groin.

Treatment: No cure. Acyclovir (Zovirax), valcyclovir (Valtrex), and famcyclovir (Famovir) are drugs that can be taken to treat the first outbreak and to reduce the number and severity of future occurrences. One recent study shows that taking daily valcyclovir can decrease the spread of the virus from an infected person to an uninfected person.

If Untreated: Individuals with herpes may have prolonged outbreaks and even more severe symptoms. However, over the years (even without medication), outbreaks tend to occur less frequently and to be less severe.

A pregnant woman who has new, active herpes sores on her vagina or cervix at the time of delivery risks spreading the virus to her baby during childbirth. Infected people should not have sex while herpes sores are present, because of the increased risk of infecting their partners. However, the herpes virus is often transmitted when no sores are present and there is no feeling that sores are about to break out.

5. Human Papilloma (pap - il - o - ma) Virus (HPV)

Several types of HPV cause genital warts. Genital warts are the most common viral STD in the United States, and they result in over 1 million health care provider visits per year. Close to half of all sexually active teens have been infected with HPV. Some types of HPV can cause pre-cancerous changes in the cells of the surface of the cervix. For this reason, it is important for all teenagers to get an annual pap smears within three years of becoming sexually active. You are a more likely to get HPV if you:

- started having sex at an early age (whether by choice or forced)
- have multiple sex partners
- don't use condoms regularly (although condoms do not provide 100% protection against HPV or HSV)

Genital warts caused by HPV are usually diagnosed by seeing warts on the genitals during an exam. Changes on Pap smears often suggest that there may be a HPV infection of the cervix. In young people, many of the mildly abnormal cells of the cervix caused by HPV improve with time so avoiding unneccessary treatment is often the safest thing to do as long as you are getting close follow up with your health care provider.

Symptoms: Warts are sometimes not visible for 3 months to a year after infection. When they appear, they are usually painless bumps or cauliflower-like growths around the anus, vulvar area, penis, or urethra. The only way to find out if HPV has caused changes to the cells of the cervix is to get a pap smear.

Treatment: No treatment can totally get rid of HPV; the virus may either stay in your body for the rest of your life, or your body may clear away the virus by your immune system. Visible warts can be removed by burning, freezing, or lasering them off, or through surgery. A health care provider can apply trichloroacetic acid (TCA) to warts over time, at a number of office visits, to remove warts. A newer medication called Imiquimod (Aldara) Cream can be put on the warts three times a week for 8-12 weeks, and over time the warts shrink or go away.

If Untreated: HPV may lead to cervical dysplasia and cancer of the cervix or penis. There are specific tests your health care provider can do to determine which type of HPV you have, and whether or not it is the type that causes cancer. All women with genital warts should have an annual pap smear. Even if you can't see the warts, the virus can be spread from one partner to another. Therefore, you need to use condoms (but remember that condoms are not 100% effective at preventing the spread of HPV).

6. Hepatitis B
Hepatitis B is caused by the hepatitis B virus (HBV). As with the other viral infections, there is no cure for hepatitis B. An estimated 150,000 new cases of HBV infection are transmitted sexually each year. Hepatitis B infection is usually diagnosed by a blood test.

Symptoms: Nausea, vomiting, stomach pain, headache, fever, yellow skin (jaundice), dark urine, liver tenderness.

Treatment: Hepatitis B has no cure. A vaccine, given in a series of three shots over 6 months, is available to prevent infection. If you have not gotten your Hepatitis B shot, talk to your health care provider.

If Untreated: Hepatitis B can lead to chronic, persistent, active hepatitis, cirrhosis, liver cancer, liver failure, and even death.

7. Pubic Lice or Crabs

Pubic lice are tiny parasitic organisms that look like insects, with segmented torsos and claws for clinging to hair. They may be passed from person to person by many kinds of close contact, both sexual and non-sexual. Slightly more women than men become infested with pubic lice. Pubic lice are usually diagnosed by being seen under a good light during a physical exam.

Symptoms: Lice can cause irritation ranging from slight discomfort to severe itching in the pubic area, although sometimes people have lice and have no symptoms. Nits (clear white egg sacs on the hair) or adult lice may be seen on pubic hairs, and the lice might leave a fine, rust-colored powder on your underwear.

Treatment: Over-the-counter medications in the form of crème rinses or shampoos such as Nix® and Rid® are commonly used. Shaving off your pubic hair will not cure lice but it will make you even itchier! It is extremely important to wash all the clothing and bedding used by a person who has lice so they do not get re-infected.

If Untreated: Pubic lice cause no permanent damage, just lots of itching

8. Trichomonas (trick - oh - MOH - nas) or "Trich"

Trichomonas is caused by infection of the vagina, urethra, or the urinary tract by trichomonas vaginalis, a microscopic protozoan organism. Trichomonas is usually diagnosed by examining a woman's vaginal fluid or a man's urine under a microscope.

Symptoms: Symptoms differ slightly for men and women:
- **men** – burning with urination, frequent urination, discharge from penis, a "tickling" feeling in the penis,
- **women** – vaginal discharge, itching and burning in vaginal-vulva area, fishy or unpleasant vaginal odor, vaginal spotting.

Treatment: A single dose of an oral antibiotic called metronidazole or Flagyl. Though very effective at killing trichomonas, this medication can make you violently ill if taken within 24 hours of drinking alcohol and you should not drink alcohol at least 24 hours after your last metronidazole tablet.

If Untreated: Men may develop prostate problems, women may have heavy, uncomfortable discharge and an increased risk of PID (see page 156).

9. Syphilis (SIFF - I - lis)
Syphilis is a bacterial infection caused by Treponema pallidium. One of the most serious of all STDs, syphilis causes permanent damage if not diagnosed and treated early. Every year, about 40,000 people in the U.S. get primary and secondary syphilis. Recent syphilis outbreaks have been linked with the exchange of sex for drugs, especially crack cocaine. Because of a link between syphilis and HIV infection, you should have a HIV test if you are diagnosed with syphilis. Syphilis is usually diagnosed by a blood test.

Symptoms: Vary according to stage of disease:
- **primary** – a painless sore (chancre) on the vulva or penis
- **secondary** – skin rash, lymph node enlargement
- **latent** – no visible (surface) symptoms, serious internal damage, may last for several years.

Treatment: Antibiotics, such as a shot of penicillin. If treated early, syphilis will not cause permanent damage.

If Untreated: Syphilis will reach its third stage after many years of infection, causing serious problems such as neurological problems, dementia, blindness, deafness, heart disease, aneurysms, and brain damage.

10. Pelvic Inflammatory Disease (PID)
PID is often caused by untreated infections such as Chlamydia and gonorrhea, but other non-sexually transmitted bacteria can also cause PID. This disease used to lead to nearly 225,000

hospitalizations every year in the United States, but today's treatment of PID is much different. Now, most women who are treated for PID are not hospitalized, but rather are given either a shot of an antibiotic plus 14 days of an oral antibiotic, or two oral antibiotics to take for 14 days. It is very important that a woman avoid repeat PID infections. With each repeated episode of PID, the chances of becoming infertile (unable to get pregnant) more than doubles. PID can cause infertility by scarring the fallopian tubes.

Table X: PID and Infertility*

Prevelance of PID in women infected with cervical gonorrhea:
      40% if gonorrhea untreated
      0% if gonorrhea adequately treated

Percentage of women who become infertile after each episode of PID:
      1st – 11%
      2nd – 23%
      3rd – 54%

PID is more likely to happen to women who:
   • are under the age of 24
   • have multiple sex partners
   • have a partner with multiple sex partners
   • have had PID in the past
   • douche (see page 38)
   • have bacterial vaginosis (See next section)
   • are in the first 5 days of their menstrual cycle

11. Bacterial Vaginosis or "BV"
BV is caused by an overgrowth of a unhealthy bacteria in the vagina. It is more common in sexually active women and it is considered to be sexually associated, but it is not considered to be a STD. That means that the male partner of a woman with BV does not need to be treated. BV is more common in women who douche and is believed to be a cause of PID. BV can also cause pre-term labor in pregnant women.

Symptoms:
In Women: vaginal discharge, fishy or unpleasant vaginal odor

Treatment: An oral antibiotic called metronidazole or Flagyl can be taken twice a day for 7 days. There are also two vaginal products, metronidazole gel or clindamycin cream that can also be used to treat BV. Despite treatment, BV often comes back.

If untreated: women may have a heavy, smelly discharge and an increased risk of PID

Prevention: The NuvaRing contraceptive ring may decrease the incidence of BV.

PREVENTING THE SPREAD OF STDS
After reading about all these STDs and their often painful results, you may wonder how anyone aware of these facts can enjoy sex. However, many pleasurable activities have risk factors, such as driving a car, eating red meat, and drinking a glass of wine. Sex, as with any activity, can bring you both pleasure and pain. Careless behaviors can easily tip the scales, causing more pain than pleasure. The smart driver wears a seat belt and drives within the speed limit; the wise meat-eater balances his or her diet; the healthy drinker drinks only moderately and not before driving a car or making important decisions. While learning to have safer sex may seem more complicated than these other activities, safer behaviors can become a habit. Simple steps can be taken to reduce the risk of unintended pregnancy and STDs. While abstinence is the only way to assure 100% protection, there are ways to be sexually active and safe. This list can help you decide what steps you can take to live a healthier and safer life.

How safe are you? How safe can you be?
"Safer sex" practices suggested for reducing the risk of getting STDs* are as follows:

Safe
- massages
- hugging
- body rubbing
- kissing (dry)

- masturbation
- hand to genital touching (hand job)
- mutual masturbation

Possibly Safe
- kissing (wet)
- vaginal/anal intercourse using latex or polyurethane condom
- oral intercourse on a man using a latex or polyurethane condom
- oral intercourse on a woman, who does not have her period or a vaginal infection with discharge, using a latex or polyurethane barrier, such as a dam (see next section on page 160), for extra safety

Unsafe
- any sex without a latex or polyurethane condom
- oral sex on a man without a latex or polyurethane condom
- oral sex on a woman, during her period or who has a vaginal infection, without a latex or polyurethane barrier (dam)
- oral-anal contact without a latex or polyurethane barrier
- sharing sex toys or douching equipment (unless they are covered by a latex or polyurethane condom)
- blood contact of ANY kind, including menstrual blood, sharing needles, and any sex that causes skin damage or bleeding

Reference: Extensive references on HIV Infection and AIDS, as well as other STDs, may be found in Contraceptive Technology 2004. This book may be purchased at www.ManagingContraception.com.

Protecting Yourself from Sexually Transmitted Infections

Although it is important to consider which methods might work best for preventing pregnancy, it is also important to think about preventing STDs. As you probably already know, the best way to prevent pregnancy and STDs is abstinence (not having intercourse). There are still many ways to be sexual, feel close to your partner, and show that you care without having the kind of sex that involves the risks of STDs or pregnancy. These would include hugging, kissing with your mouth opened or closed, massage (rubbing your partner or your partner rubbing you), and masturbation (touching yourself and your partner touching him/

herself for pleasure, or touching each other in ways that you both enjoy). These sexual activities are safe as long as the touching does not involve blood, semen (cum), or vaginal fluids.

See section on Male and Female Condoms in Part 2, pages 92 and 98 for more on preventing STDs during vaginal or anal intercourse.

To protect yourself and your partner from getting an infection when you have oral sex, it is a good idea to use a dental dam (sometimes called a latex dam). A dam is a square of latex or polyurethane (a type of plastic). It is put on top of the outside of the vagina (vulva) or anus (also called the rectum) during oral sex to protect both partners from infections. Each dam should only be used once and then thrown out. Dental dams help to reduce the risk of passing the HIV infection during oral-vaginal and oral-anal sex, in addition to other diseases that can be passed from mouth to vulva/anus or vice-versa, including herpes and genital warts.

How effective is a dental dam?
When used properly, dams provide an effective barrier to bodily fluids during oral sexual activity. Dental dams can significantly reduce the risk of contact with a sexually transmitted disease, but they are not 100% effective. Only abstinence is 100% effective. To use a dam, open the package and carefully remove the dam. Be careful if you have sharp fingernails or nail jewelry, so you don't tear the dam. Unfold it and lay it over the genitals (vulva or anus) before any oral contact. Put a drop of lube underneath the dam (against the skin) for increased sensation and comfort.

If the person giving oral sex has braces or oral piercings (on the tongue, lips, or cheeks), be careful not to tear the dam while it is being used. If a tear occurs, throw out the dam and get a new one before continuing to have oral sex. Also, be careful if the dam is dropped during oral sex, because it will be impossible to tell which side was on the person's mouth and which side was on the genitals. You can mark one side of the dam with a letter that will help you remember which side goes where. For example, you could use a "B" on the "Body" side. If you don't pre-mark the dam and drop it, throw it out and get another one before continuing.

Once you are finished, throw the dam out in the garbage. Do not flush used dams down the toilet because they can clog the pipes. **Dams can only be used once.**

How much does a dam cost, and where can you get one?
Dental dams run from $0.50 - $3.00 each, depending on size, color, flavor, etc. Buying a multi-pack makes them cheaper. Dams may be hard to find, but you can usually get them from health care providers or larger drug stores. Dental dams are not always available in drug stores or pharmacies. It may be necessary to ask for them or order online:
www.sheerglydedams.com
www.justrubbers.com
www.drcondoms.com
www.condom.com

What do I do if I can't find dental dams in the stores?
If you have trouble finding dams, you can use other materials to protect you and your partner. Dental dams can be made out of condoms, latex gloves, or Saran Wrap, so you can get the makings of one almost anywhere. For making dams out of condoms, is better to use flavored or non-lubricated kinds. However, if you only have a lubricated condom, first wash the lubricant off of the condom with lukewarm water. Next, cut the tip off and cut up the side of the rolled condom. Unroll the sheet of latex and place over the vagina or anus. It is important not to use condoms that have nonoxynol-9 or other spermicidal lubricants, because the spermicide may irritate the mouth or genitals and can increase your risk of getting an STD.

Dental dams can be made from condoms with two easy snips as shown to the right.
If you don't have a dam or a condom, you can use plastic wrap (Saran wrap) to make a dam. You can only use non-microwavable wrap, because the kind you use in the microwave has small holes that might allow viruses and bacteria to pass through – so read the label carefully! Rip off a piece large enough to cover the

whole genital area (the vagina, labia, clitoris and anus).

Advantages: Dental dams...
- Come in flavors and colors designed to make oral intercourse more pleasurable and exciting.
- Provide a new and unique sensation.
- Offer some protection against oral transmission of sexually transmitted diseases.

Disadvantages: Dental dams...
- Do not protect against pregnancy, as they are not intended to be used for anal or vaginal intercourse.
- May take away some of the sensation.

Must be held in place at all times, which means someone's hands are not free. To reduce this challenge some dams are made with adhesive so they stick in place, and both people are then free to move their hands wherever they want. Otherwise, you can use one of your hands and one of your partner's hands to hold the dam, or you can purchase a small harness to hold the dam in place, called a "dammit."

QUESTIONS TEENAGERS ASK ABOUT SEX*

Do girls have anything like an erection?
Girls do not get erections the way boys do. But girls do have a part of their genitals - the clitoris, the labia and the mons swell slightly during arousal. It feels similar to the pleasurable feelings that boys get in their penises. The clitoris is much smaller than a penis, but it fills up with blood when a girl is sexually excited, in much the same way as the penis does when a boy is sexually excited. Most women experience a wetness in the vagina, called lubrication, when they feel sexually aroused. Wetness is a "signal" in a woman that she is turned on - much like an erection in a man.

What is the normal size for a penis?
There is no such thing as a penis that is too short or too long. Whatever size penis a boy or man has is normal for him. Besides, when a penis is erect, it's almost always big enough to please both partners.

If sex is so great, and your body is ready, why do so many parents say it's wrong for teenagers to do it?
Although your body may be physically ready to have sexual intercourse, your parents are worried about the emotional consequences of very early sexual behavior. Your parents understand that it's normal to have sexual feelings at your age, but they also want you to know that a mature, grown-up relationship is built on other things besides sex, including respect for, and understanding of, the other person's feelings. You need to feel good about yourself first, so that you can cope with the consequences of sexual activity - which means being responsible about birth control and protecting yourself from sexually transmitted diseases, as well as coping if or when your relationship should end.

Should a boy use a condom if he's having sex with a virgin?
Yes. A girl who's a virgin can still get pregnant the first time she has sexual intercourse, especially if a reliable method of birth control is not used. This is exactly what happens every day in the United States. A condom is the most reliable means

of protection against sexually transmitted infections (other than abstinence) and it is also very effective as a contraceptive if used correctly each and every time.

My friend told me that taking a bath or douching right after having sex can help wash out the sperm and prevent pregnancy. Is she right?

No. It's impossible for a woman to wash out sperm completely after a man ejaculates (cums) inside her. This is because the sperm swim so quickly into the womb (or uterus) that before she can sit up, odds are that some of the sperm have already reached her fallopian tubes, where they may meet an egg. Although douching may help a little, it is not effective enough to be considered a form of birth control. Also, douching can cause a smelly vaginal bacterial infection, called BV. Douching can also push an infection up into a woman's uterus and cause PID

Can a girl get pregnant if she hasn't started getting her periods yet?

Yes. Although girls who have not started getting menstrual periods may not yet be ovulating regularly, there have been reports of girls getting pregnant when they had sex before they started having periods. Once your breasts and pubic hair have developed, your body can start to ovulate and menstruate at any time.

Can a girl get pregnant if she has sex during her menstrual period?

Yes. Most girls ovulate in the middle of their menstrual cycle, about 14 days before they start their next period. However, not all bleeding from the vagina is from a period (infections can cause bleeding) and not all girls ovulate at the same time. There is really no completely safe time of the menstrual cycle to have sex and guarantee you will not get pregnant.

If a man withdraws his penis just before he ejaculates, won't it keep the woman from getting pregnant?

Not necessarily. In fact, it's risky. Small amounts of semen, the fluid that contains sperm, may leak out before the man ejaculates, so there is still a danger of sperm coming in contact with the egg - meaning the woman can still get pregnant. Also, there is still a risk of STD infection with this method. But even withdrawal is a much better method than no method at all.

Does urinating after sex protect a woman from getting pregnant?
Don't believe this one! Urinating has nothing to do with preventing pregnancy. Urine leaves a woman's body from a different opening than the one sperm travel through to get to the uterus. She can't "flush" out sperm by going to the bathroom. However, urinating after sex can reduce a woman's chances of getting a bladder infection.

How can a person tell if he or she is truly allergic to latex condoms?
When a person is allergic to latex condoms, they may get redness, swelling or a burning sensation around the penis or the labia and vagina after using a latex condom. The first thing you can do is check the condom package and see if the condom was lubricated with spermicide; it may be the spermicide that is causing the irritation. You can also try using an non-lubricated condom with a separate lubricant like Astroglide® or KY Jelly®. If that doesn't work, try a polyurethane condom (made of a type of plastic) like Avanti® or Supra®.

How old must a girl be to go on the Pill?
There is no particular age when it is "right" for a girl to go on the Pill, or get any other method of birth control. The "right" time to think about birth control is when she decides to have sexual intercourse or before she first has intercourse. Then, it is important for her to choose a birth control method that she feels comfortable with and will be willing to use every time she has intercourse. It's best to make the decision about which contraceptive to use after getting advice from a doctor or nurse practitioner.

I've heard that the Pill can give you cancer. Is this true?
There is no current evidence that today's birth control pills are linked to an increase in any form of cancer. The Pill is very safe for healthy women who don't smoke - including teenagers and women over forty years of age. In fact, the Pill actually can help protect a woman against two very important types of cancer,

cancer of the ovary and cancer of the lining of the uterus.

Can a woman feel a vaginal ring once it is inside her?
If she has put the ring in properly, a woman will not know it's there, and neither will her partner.

Can you get AIDS from a dirty toilet seat in a public rest room?
No. HIV, the virus that causes AIDS, can be transmitted only through contact with body fluids, such as blood, semen, or vaginal fluids of someone who has the virus. You cannot get HIV or other STDs from a toilet seat or from other forms of casual contact, such as hugging or holding hands with someone who has the virus.

Can you get AIDS by kissing someone who has the virus?
It is highly unlikely that you would get HIV - the virus that causes AIDS - by kissing someone who is infected, even though HIV has been found, in very small numbers, in saliva. In fact, most researchers say that no one has gotten HIV through kissing. However, it is possible that the virus could be passed if you have an open cut or sore in your mouth (which you can get after brushing or flossing). Health care providers advise that both partners avoid brushing or flossing your teeth before kissing so that no blood is present. Also, don't have oral sex unless you use a condom or other form of protection.

I've heard a lot of talk about "safe sex." What exactly does this mean?
Well, if you are talking about sexual intercourse - vaginal, oral, or anal - there's probably no such thing as completely safe sex. However, there are completely safe ways of being sexual without intercourse. For example, hugging, body massage, and masturbation are all ways of being sexual that don't lead to pregnancy or STDs. There are also ways of having safer intercourse. Couples who decide to have sexual intercourse should use a latex condom or other barriers to prevent contact with body fluids such as semen, blood, and vaginal fluids.

Doesn't birth control make sex less romantic?
Although some people believe this, it is not usually so. For example, a woman can put in a diaphragm several hours before

she has sexual intercourse. Some people also like to incorporate birth control into their lovemaking. For example, a man can help a woman put in her diaphragm or spermicide, or a woman can put the condom on her partner.

How do I get that sticky grey ring from my old Evra patch site off my skin?
Rubbing baby oil or a moisturizer on your skin where the old patch was should take that sticky adhesive right off. But make sure you do not put oils on your skin when trying to stick a new patch on, or it will not stick!

I'm afraid of getting pregnant, so my boyfriend and I have oral sex. Is there any risk of getting pregnant or getting a STDs from oral sex?
While there is no risk of pregnancy from oral sex, it is still possible to get a sexually transmitted disease (STD) through oral sex. All STDs including HIV can be transmitted by putting the mouth on the penis, vagina or anus. If you decide to have oral sex, it is best to use a latex or polyurethane (a type of plastic) barrier to protect both you and your partner. To prevent infections, a condom can be placed over the penis before any sex where the penis enters a part of the body, including the mouth. Since a condom cannot be placed over the vagina or anus, a dental dam (a square of latex or plastic) should be used.

Can my partner tell if I'm a virgin?
In some cultures, a woman who has an intact hymen (a thin piece of fleshy tissue that stretches across the vaginal opening) has "proof" that she is still a virgin; however, the hymen often enlarges or "breaks" from putting in or pulling out a tampon, vigorous exercise, or from putting a finger in the vagina. Some girls are born without a hymen! Having or not having a hymen is not a foolproof way of proving a woman is a virgin. In a man, it is impossible to tell because there is no physical sign of virginity. If you want to know if your partner is a virgin or had any type of sexual activities in the past, the best way to find out is to ask him/her.

I'm a 15-year-old boy and I like other boys, does that mean that I have AIDS?
Who you feel physically or sexually attracted to have nothing to do with HIV or AIDS! It is what you do sexually that puts you at risk, not your sexual feelings. AIDS is a disease that is caused by the HIV virus and passed from person to person by touching blood, semen or vaginal secretions.

I want to remain a virgin until I'm married, but my boyfriend wants to have sex, so I think anal sex is a good compromise. If I have anal sex, am I still a virgin?
You may want to discuss your values and beliefs with an adult you trust, like a family member, clergy member, or teacher. Doing this may help you to decide your own definition of virginity. The dictionary meaning of a virgin is someone who has not had sexual intercourse and some people define intercourse as any sexual contact. Once you have decided what is consistent with your beliefs about virginity, if you decide to have anal sex it is important to learn how to protect yourself from sexually transmitted diseases and pregnancy. Anal sex can put you and your partner at risk for sexually transmitted diseases and can also put you at some risk for pregnancy because semen often leaks into your vagina after anal intercourse. Using a latex or polyurethane (a type of plastic) condom may help prevent STDs and lessen your chances of getting pregnant.

GLOSSARY

abortion – a surgical or medical procedure during which the fetus is removed from a woman's uterus

abstinence – a sexual practice where people choose not to have intercourse

acquired immunodeficiency syndrome (AIDS) – a disease caused by the Human Immunodeficiency Virus (HIV) that attacks a person's immune system to the point where a person could die from any infection

acyclovir – an antivirus medicine used to treat herpes and prevent repeat outbreaks

alcohol – drinks or beverages contain ethanol such as beer, wine, wine coolers, malt beverages, and hard liquor

alcoholism - a disease that cause people to be unable to control their drinking

anal sex – a form of intercourse during which a man puts his penis into the anus of a woman or another man

antibiotics – medication that is used to treat or cure a bacterial infection

anti-retroviral – a type of medication used to treat HIV and other viral infections

arousal – feelings of sexual excitement or feeling "turned on"

asymptomatic – not having any symptoms or complaints

Azithromycin – An antibiotic commonly used to treat Chlamydia

benign breasts masses – non-cancerous tumor found in the breast

binge drinking – drinking a certain number of drinks at one sitting. For men, drinking 5 or more drinks at a sitting is considered a binge; for women, 4 or more drinks is considered a binge

blackout – when a person passes out and/or does not remember what happened to them; usually occurs when one is drunk on alcohol or high of drugs

breast cancer – an abnormal tissue growth in the breast

breast self-examination (BSE) – a way that a woman feels for abnormal lumps or a thickening in the breast and armpits, once a month, usually right after her period

cervical cancer – an abnormal, malignant growth of cells from the surface of the cervix

cervical dysplasia – Pre-cancerous abnormal cells form the surface of the cervix

cervical mucus – a normal discharge made by the cervix that drains from the vagina to the outside of the body

cervical cap – a small latex or silicone cap that covers the cervix. Used with spermicidal jelly or cream to prevent pregnancy

cervix – the lower portion, of the uterus, that stick out into the upper portion of the vagina. The cervix opens during labor to allow passage of the infant from the uterus

chancre – a painless sore that forms on the genitals and/or the mouth. These sores can be a symptom of certain STDs

cirrhosis – a disease of the liver that can be caused by drinking a lot of alcohol over time

clitoris – a small, pea sized, hooded, erectile tissue located on the top of the vulva above the vagina. Like the male's penis it is highly sensitive to sexual stimulation

condom – a pouch-shaped covering of latex, plastic, or sheep intestine worn over the penis during intercourse to prevent pregnancy and the transmission of STDs

corpus luteum – Cells in the ovary that make hormones that regulate ovulation and menstruation

cunnilingus – oral sex performed on a woman

date rape – when a friend or partner forces you to have intercourse when you do not want to

dementia – loss of the ability to think and process ideas normally

dental dam – a latex or polyurethane (plastic) square that is put over the vagina or anus to protect against STDs during oral sex

Depo-Provera® - progestin injections given every 3 months to prevent pregnancy

depression – the state of being sad and lonely, a cause of suicide in teenagers

diaphragm – a soft rubber dome-shaped cup worn in the vagina in front of the cervix and used with spermicidal jelly or cream for the prevention of pregnancy

discharge – fluid from the vagina or the penis.

douching – rinsing out the vagina with fluid

doxycycline – an antibiotic used to treat bacterial sexually transmitted infections

ectopic (tubal) pregnancy – when the fertilized egg implants (sticks) someplace other than the lining of the uterus, usually in the fallopian tubes

ejaculation – semen released from a man's penis, also called "cum" or "coming"

endometrial cancer – cancer of the lining of uterus

endometrium – the inner lining of the uterus

epididymis – the soft tubing attached to the testicles, where sperm matures and is stored prior to ejaculation

erection – when the penis gets hard as it fills up with blood during sexual excitement

erogenous zones – sensitive areas of the body that can be sexually aroused by touch, such as the penis, clitoris, thighs, buttocks, breasts, nipples, neck and ears

estrogen – the primary female sex hormone made by the ovary that is responsible for developing a female's body during puberty

etiquette – suggested rules or guidelines of appropriate behavior

excitement stage – first stage of the sexual response cycle where a person is sexually aroused, stimulated or "turned on"

fallopian tubes – delicate 4 inch tubes or ducts through which an egg travels from the ovary to the uterus, and through which sperm move from the uterus towards the ovary

fellatio – oral sex performed on a man

fertilization – when the sperm and egg meet and join

fibroids – non-cancerous tumors or growths of the muscle and connective tissues of the uterus

follicle stimulating hormone – a hormone from the pituitary gland that stimulates the ovaries to ripen egg follicles in women and stimulates the testicles to make sperm in men

foreplay – kissing, teasing, caressing, and massaging to get "turned on" before, or instead of, intercourse

French kissing – a type of kissing where two people touch tongue to tongue or put a tongue in another person's mouth

gender identity – your experience of how you feel on the inside - male or female or a mixture of both; usually develops when you are a child

genes – the elements or chromosomes that you inherit from your parents which determine certain characteristics

hallucinogens – substances that cause a person to see, hear, or feel imaginary things

hepatitis – inflammation of the liver that can be from infections or injury from drugs or alcohol

herpes – a virus that causes sores on the genitals and mouth that remains with a person for life

heterosexuality – when a person is physically or sexually attracted to someone of the opposite sex

homosexuality – when a person is physically or sexually attracted to someone of the same sex

hormone – chemical messengers made by a gland that changes how a body organ works

human chorionic gonadotropin (HCG) – a hormone that is made during pregnancy that can be measured in the blood or urine to test for pregnancy

human papilloma virus (HPV) – a virus that causes genital warts and some types of cervical and penis cancer

human immunodeficiency virus (HIV) – the virus that causes AIDS

implantation – when a fertilized egg sticks to the lining of the uterus

inhalants – drugs that can be inhaled (breathed in) such as sprays and vapors

infertility – inability to get pregnant or get someone pregnant

intercourse – a range of sexual interactions between two people

intrauterine device (IUD) – a flexible, usually plastic device inserted into the uterus to prevent pregnancy

jaundice – yellowing of the eyes and skin usually because of an inflammation of the liver

latex – type of rubber used in making condoms, dental dams, diaphragms, and some cervical caps

lubrication – increased natural wetness coming from the vagina

lubricant –any liquid used to make sex more slippery and more comfortable; can be put on the penis, vagina, on a condom or on the anus before and during sex.

luteinizing hormone – a hormone made by the pituitary gland that causes ovulation (release of a ripe egg from the ovary). In the male it stimulates the testicles to make testosterone and sperm cells

lymph node – small glands in the neck, armpits and groin that are part of the immune system

masturbation – when a person stimulates his or her own sex organs or body for sexual pleasure

menstrual cramps – a type of lower abdominal pain that usually occurs during the first few days of each menstrual period; may be relived by over the counter medication like ibuprofen or naproxen sodium

menstrual cycle - A menstrual cycle is the period of time from the start of one bleeding period to the start of the next; the average cycle length is 28 days.

menstruation – when the lining of the uterus comes off, usually monthly when a woman is not pregnant

mittelschmerz – pain that happens during the middle of the cycle associated with ovulation

morning after pill – hormone pills that can prevent pregnancy after unprotected sex if taken within 5 days after intercourse, also called emergency contraception

mutual masturbation – when two people stimulate each others' sex organs at the same time

narcotics – drugs such as cocaine, oxycontin, Demerol, and heroin

Norplant® – six silicon rods that are inserted into a woman's upper arm that release a hormone to prevent pregnancy

orgasm – the third stage of the sexual response cycle where a man ejaculates (comes) and a woman has contractions of her vaginal and pelvic muscles

oral contraceptives – hormone pills taken by mouth once a day to prevent pregnancy

oral sex – when a person puts his/her mouth or tongue on his/her partner's genitals (clitoris, vagina, penis, anus) for pleasure

ovarian cancer – a tumor growing in a woman's ovaries that is cancerous

ovarian cysts – fluid filled spaces that form in the ovaries

ovaries – organs that make eggs and hormones like estrogen and progesterone in a woman.

ovulation – the point when a ripe egg is released from the ovary during the female menstrual cycle

pap smear – a screening test where cells collected from the surface of the cervix are placed onto a slide or liquid-filled container, to be examined under a microscope; used to detect cancer of the cervix

parasite – an organism that lives off another organism; examples include pubic lice and trichomonas

pelvic exam – An examination of the female sex organs including the external genitalia (pubic area, vulva, labia, the opening of the vagina or introitus, clitoris, perineum, urethra), vagina, cervix, uterus, fallopian tubes, and ovaries

pelvic inflammatory disease (PID) – inflammation of the upper genital tract, including the uterus and the tubes, often caused by STDs

pelvic mass – tumor found in the pelvic region

penis – male external sexual organ

pharynx – the back of the throat

phencyclidine – also called PCP; a drug that causes hallucinations

pituitary gland – a small gland in the brain that makes hormones that regulate the menstrual cycle in women and sperm production in men

plateau stage – second stage of the sexual response cycle where orgasm seems inevitable; changes in the body that begin in the excitement stage increase during the plateau stage and can last from minutes to sometimes hours

premenstrual syndrome (PMS) – unpleasant physical and emotional experiences that happen prior to the menstrual period

progesterone – a hormone made in the ovaries during the latter half of the menstrual cycle that changes the lining of the uterus and prepares it for a fertilized egg

progestin – a type of man-made hormone similar to one made by the ovary in the latter half of the menstrual cycle after ovulation. see progesterone

prostate – the gland in the man that makes semen, a fluid that is ejaculated with sperm

protease inhibitors – a type of medication to treat HIV infections

puberty – hormonal and physical changes that occur between the ages of 9 and 17 that result in the body reaching mature, adult shape and function

rape – any sexual activity involving penetration of the vagina and/or anus, and/or oral contact with the genitals that is forced by either physical or verbal threats.

scrotum – the bag or sack that hangs below the penis that holds a man's testicles

sedatives – drugs that decreases irritability, nervousness, or excitement and make you sleepy

self-esteem – feeling confident and satisfied in one's self

semen – the thick, whitish fluid that has sperm in it that is released during ejaculation

serotonin – a chemical in the brain associated with good moods; some types of depression may be caused by not having enough of this chemical

sexual abuse – any form of sexual contact or harassment that is against someone's wishes; may include physical violence, coercion, or verbal threats

sexual assault – any form of sexual force or coerced sexual contact

sexual orientation – feelings of physical attraction that help a person to define who he or she is as a sexual being

sexual intercourse – a very physical and intimate kind of sex between two people; the three different kinds of intercourse include vaginal (penis-in-vagina), anal (penis-in-anus), and oral (mouth-to-penis, mouth-to-vagina, mouth-to-anus)

sexually transmitted diseases (STDs) – infections that can be passed from person to person through sexual contact

speculum – an instrument used for holding open the walls of the vagina so one can look at and take swabs from the vagina or the cervix

sperm – male reproductive cell made in the testicles

spermicide – a chemical substance that kills sperm, and is put inside the vagina, on diaphragms or cervical caps or on condoms, Come in the form of cream, foam, jelly, suppositories, and film

stimulants – drugs that excite a person's body

suppositories – bullet-shaped birth control method containing spermicides that is put into the vagina prior to intercourse

symptoms – physical or psychological complaints

T-4 lymphocytes – cells in the blood that protect against foreign bodies. These are the cells attacked by the HIV virus

testicles – the organs in a man that produce sperm and testosterone

testicular self examination (TSE) – a way for the male to check himself for any abnormal lumps in the testes

testosterone – the sex hormone that is responsible for the development of a man's body during puberty. This is also a hormone women's bodies make.

tetracycline – (see doxycycline)

toxic shock syndrome (TSS) – a severe illness that has a sudden high fever, vomiting, diarrhea, aches, and a sunburn like rash that may lead to death. Often associated with leaving a tampon in the vagina too long.

urethra – a tube which drains urine from the bladder, to the outside of the body. In women the opening of the urethra is between the clitoris and the vagina. For men, the urethra transports semen to the outside of the body

uterus – a hollow, pear-shaped, muscular, elastic reproductive organ where the fetus develops during pregnancy

vagina – a 3 to 5 inch long muscular tube leading from the external genitals of the female to the cervix. Also called the birth canal

vaginal canal – (see vagina)

vaginal contraceptive film – thin spermicidal sheet that can, when placed in the vagina, prevent pregnancy

vas deferens – tubes that carry sperm from the testes to the urethra

wet dream – an erotic dream that end in ejaculation of semen

withdrawal – a method of preventing pregnancy when the man removes his penis from the woman's vagina right before ejaculation

Resources

Books For Young People

Hatcher RA, Trussell J, Stewart F, et al. Contraceptive Technology: Eighteenth Revised Edition. Ardent Media Inc, NY, 2004.

Hatcher RA, Colestock S, Pluhar E, Thrasher C. Sexual Etiquette 101, 4th edition. The Bridging the Gap, Dawsonville, GA, 2001.

Bell R. Changing Bodies, Changing Lives: Expanded Third Edition: A Book for Teens on Sex and Relationships. Three Rivers Press, NY, NY (Paperback -- 1998).

Rutledge JZ. Dealing with stuff that makes life tough: 10 things that stress teen girls out and how to cope with them. 2003

Basso MJ. The Underground Guide to Teen Sexuality: An Essential Handbook for Today's Teens & Parents. Fairview Press, 2003.

Drill E, Mcdonald H, Odes R. Deal with It! A Whole New Approach to Your Body, Brain, and Life as a Gurl. Pocketbooks, Division of Simon and Schuster, Inc. 1999

Books for Your Parents

Godfrey R. The Teen Code: How to Talk to Them about Sex, Drugs, and Everything Else--Teenagers Reveal What Works Best. Rodale, Inc., 2004.

Richardson J and Schuster MA. Everything You Never Wanted Your Kids to Know About Sex, but Were Afraid They'd Ask: The Secrets to Surviving Your Child's Sexual Development from Birth to the Teens. Crown Publisher, Division of Random House, Inc. NY, NY, 2003.

Telephone Numbers

American College Health Association
    (302) 963-1100

American Respiratory Alliance (to stop smoking cigarettes)
    1-800-220-1990

Emergency Contraception Hotline
    1-888-NOT-2-LATE (toll free)

ETR (Education, Training, Research)
    1-800-321-4407

Free Quit Line (to stop smoking cigarettes)
    1-877-724-1090 (toll free)

Gay Men's Health Crisis
    (212) 807-6655

Incest Survivors Information Exchange
    (203) 255-5192

National AIDS Hotline
    1-800-342-2437
    1-800-243-7889 for hearing impaired
    1-800-344-7472 or 7432 for Spanish Access
    1-800-234-8336 for teenagers

National Abortion Federation (NAF) Hotline
    1-800-772-9100

National Association for Children of Alcoholics (NACOA)
    (714) 299-3889

National Child Abuse Hotline
    1-800-4-A-CHILD (1-800-422-4453)
    1-800-2-A-CHILD (1-800-222-4453) for hearing impaired

National Coalition Against Sexual Assault
    (202) 483-7165

National STD Hotline
     1-800-227-8922

National Women's Health Network
     (202) 347-1140

Parents and Friends of Lesbians and Gays (PFLAG)
     (202) 638-4200

Planned Parenthood
     1-800-230-PLAN (7526)

INTERNET RESOURCES

General Teen-Friendly Websites

http://www.goaskalice.columbia.edu
http://www.teenhealth.org
http://www.advocatesforyouth.org
http://www.whatudo.org
http://www.talkingwithkids.org
http://www.youngwomenshealth.org
http://www.4woman.gov
http://www.promotetruth.org
http://www.tolerance.org
http://www.Teenwire.com
http://www.slangsite.com
http://www.ManagingContraception.com

Websites by topics

Abuse (physical, sexual and emotional), Rape and Incest
http://www.teencentral.net
http://www.rainn.org
http://www.paar.net
http://www.safeyouth.org
http://odp.webwombat.com.au/WW468881.HTM
http://endabuse.org

Alcohol and Other Drugs
http://www.al-anon-alteen.org
http://www.casacolumbia.org
http://www.freevibe.com
http://teens.drugabuse.gov
http://www.afterschool.gov/tnsubst.html

Depression and Suicide
http://www.teenlineonline.org
http://www.befrienders.org
http://www.wpic.pitt.edu/research/city
http://www.nami.org
http://www.dbsalliance.org
http://www.teenadviceonline.org
http://www.nostigma.com

Eating Disorders
http://www.nationaleatingdisorders.org
http://www.mirror-mirror.org/eatdis.htm
http://www.edauk.com
http://www.edreferral.com
http://www.anred.com
http://www.nedic.ca

Gay/Lesbian/Bisexual/Transgender Issues
http://www.glsen.org
http://www.pflag.org
http://www.ngltf.org
http://www.biresource.org
http://www.ren.org
http://www.lgbtcenters.org
http://www.lambda.org
http://www.glbthealth.org
http://www.glbtjews.org

Hobbies
http://www.bgca.org
http://www.tygo.com/dir/kids_and_teens/Hobbies_and_Sports
http://teenwriting.about.com
http://www.teenreads.com

International Youth Health
http://www.iaah.org
http://kidshealth.org/teen
http://www.ncpamd.com/Kids_Pages.htm
http://www.safekids.com

Internet Safety
http://www.getnetwise.org
http://www.safeteens.com
http://www.safekids.com
http://www.netsmartz.org
http://www.internet-safety.org

Sex, Contraception, Teen Pregnancy and STDs
http://www.siecus.org/teen
http://www.ManagingContraception.com
http://www.sxetc.org
http://www.positive.org
http://www.teenpregnancy.org
http://www.NOT-2-LATE.com
http://www.managingcontraception.com
http://www.acog.org
http://www.agi-usa.org
http://www.fhi.org
http://www.plannedparenthood.org
http://www.iwannaknow.org
http://www.safersex.org
http://www.cdcnpin.org
http://www.cdc.gov
http://www.fwhc.org
http://www.teenpregnancy.org
http://www.etr.org/recapp
http://www.awarefoundation.org
http://www.scarlateen.com

Runaways
http://www.nrscrisisline.org

Smoking Cessation (Ways to Stop Smoking)
http://www.lungusa.org
http://tobaccofreekids.org
http://kidshealth.org/teen/drug_alcohol/tobacco/smoking.html
http://www.youngwomenshealth.org/smokeinfo.html

Violence, Crime, and Harassment
http://www.apa.org/pi/pii/teen
http://www.stopthehate.org
http://www.teencentral.net
http://www.ncvc.org
http://www.ncadv.org
http://www.safeyouth.org
http://www.pavnet.org
http://www.nationaltcc.org

Other Resources Identified from the www.Teenwire.com website

Al-Anon
800-356-9996
http://www.al-anon.org
For people who need to deal with family members and friends who are recovering from alcoholism. They also sponsor Alateen, a recovery program for young people.

American Foundation for Suicide Prevention
1-800-SUICIDE
1-800-784-2433
http://www.yellowribbon.org
If you or someone you know is thinking about suicide, this is the place to go for immediate help. Learn to recognize warning signs, cope with suicidal thoughts, and get information on how to start a chapter in your area.

Childhelp USA
800-422-4453
http://www.childhelpusa.org
Every 10 seconds a child is abused. Child abuse kills more children in America than do accidental falls, drowning, choking on food, fires in the home, or suffocation. If you suspect child

abuse or need help, you can call the hotline 24 hours a day. Communication in 140 languages is available.

Children and Youth With Disabilities
800-695-0285
http://www.nichcy.org
NICHCY is the national information and referral center that provides information on disabilities and disability-related issues for families, educators, and other professionals. Their special focus is children and youth.

Freevibe
http://www.freevibe.com
This site is loaded with stats on teen drug and alcohol abuse. Send a "Buzz Bomb" to a friend, post messages on the boards, read true stories about teens with drug problems and share your own stories.

The Gay and Lesbian National Hotline
1-888-THE-GLNH
1-888-843-4564
http://www.glnh.org
If you need information, referrals, or peer-counseling and you're gay, lesbian, bisexual or transgender, this is the place for you. You can speak anonymously about your situation to someone who's trained to be an active and non-judgmental listener.

International Planned Parenthood Federation
http://www.ippf.org
This international organization fights to secure reproductive rights and provides information, counseling, and reproductive health-care services to women around the world.

likeitis
http://www.likeitis.org.uk
Cool, interactive site from the U.K. that's got info on sexuality, STIs, contraception, and more.

Making Schools Safe
http://www.aclu.org/safeschools
The ACLU's Making Schools Safe project supports LGBTQ (lesbian, gay, bisexual, transgendered, and questioning) teens who are being harassed at school because of their sexuality. Find out to to help out or fight back!

Minority Health Resource Center
800-444-6472
(en espanol)
http://www.omhrc.gov
An informative public health site which focuses on issues affecting American Indians and Alaska Natives, Asian Americans, Native Hawaiians and Other Pacific Islanders, Blacks/African Americans, and Hispanics/Latinos.

Nation One
http://www.nation1.org
Can't vote? Join this totally youth-run project that empowers young people globally using communications technologies to make a difference in the world.

National AIDS Hotline
800-342-2437
800-344-7432 (en espanol)
http://www.ashastd.org/nah/tty.html
Keep up with latest US AIDS trends. Ask your question about HIV and AIDS and read up on important things to know if you're living with HIV.

National Association of Anorexia Nervosa & Associated Disorders
847-831-3438
http://www.anad.org
Pick up free hotline counseling and learn about support groups for sufferers and families of people with eating disorders. You'll also find referrals to health care professionals who treat eating disorders across the U.S. and in fifteen other countries.

National Campaign Against Youth Violence
http://www.ncayv.org
This group encourages teens to use outlets other than violence to express themselves. The site offers tips for preventing violence and information to start anti-violence projects in your community.

National Council on Alcoholism and Drug Dependence
800-622-2255
http://www.ncadd.org
Info on substance abuse is provided on this site. Call them to get resources and services about substance use in your neighborhood.

National Health Information Center
800-336-4797
http://www.health.gov/nhic
Get connected with health professionals who can best provide answers to your health questions. Search their database for any health related issues.

National Mental Health Association
800-969-6642
http://www.nmha.org
From anxiety disorders, to depression, to attention deficit disorder, to suicide, and substance abuse — this group, with over 300 affiliates nationwide, can give a boost to anyone who feels like they might need it.

National Sexual Violence Resource Center
877-739-3895
http://www.nsvrc.org
NSVRC provides information, support, and help for victims of sexual violence. It is a project of the Pennsylvania Coalition Against Rape, which also has a site for teens that deals with sexual violence: **http://www.teenpcar.com**.

Planned Parenthood Federation of America
800-230-PLAN
http://www.plannedparenthood.org
Find great sexual health information about topics like birth control, emergency contraception, parenting and pregnancy, abortion, sexually transmitted infections and political advocacy. Or get connected with a clinic near you.

Rape, Abuse & Incest National Network
1-800-656-HOPE
http://www.rainn.org
If you have been sexually assaulted, have a friend who's been sexually assaulted, or want to know how to reduce your risk of sexual assault, RAINN's where you want to turn to.

STD Hotline
800-227-8922
http://www.ashastd.org
Find answers to frequently asked questions about sexually transmitted infections and hook up with a support group in your area.

Teen Voices
http://www.teenvoices.com
An online and print magazine by, for, and about teen girls with info on activism, the arts, and more.

The Trevor Project
1-866-4-U-TREVOR
http://www.TheTrevorProject.org
The Trevor Project is a nonprofit organization established to promote tolerance for queer and questioning teenagers, and to aid in suicide prevention among that group. The Trevor Project runs The Trevor Helpline (1-866-4-U-TREVOR) the country's first and only around-the-clock toll-free suicide prevention helpline for queer and questioning teens.